Catherine Bailey began her travels at the age of sixteen, exchanging school for Central America and the deserts of New Mexico and Arizona. She trained at RADA, launching her career in London's West End theatres, Hampstead Theatre, the National Theatre and on worldwide tours. She went on to produce for television and radio, where she won several Sony Awards. She produced David Cronenberg's movie, Spider and the hit series, The Dark is Rising, for BBC World Service. This is her first novel, based on her debut as a documentary filmmaker, shooting a film that nearly cost her life.

For my two boys, Jamie and Edward.

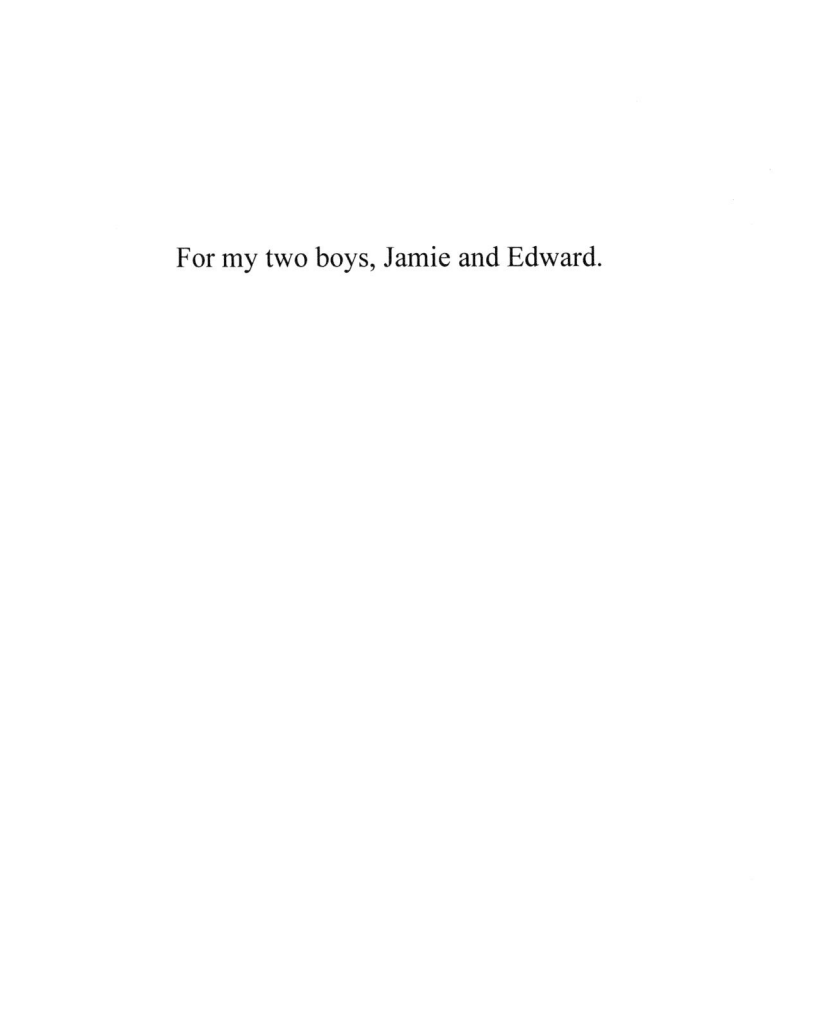

Catherine Bailey

75 MEN, A SHIPWRECK AND ME

AUSTIN MACAULEY PUBLISHERS™
LONDON * CAMBRIDGE * NEW YORK * SHARJAH

Copyright © Catherine Bailey 2024

The right of Catherine Bailey to be identified as author of this work has been asserted by the author in accordance with sections 77 and 78 of the Copyright, Designs and Patents Act 1988.

All rights reserved. No part of this publication may be reproduced, stored in a retrieval system, or transmitted in any form or by any means, electronic, mechanical, photocopying, recording, or otherwise, without the prior permission of the publishers.

Any person who commits any unauthorised act in relation to this publication may be liable to criminal prosecution and civil claims for damages.

The story, experiences, and words are the author's alone.

A CIP catalogue record for this title is available from the British Library.

ISBN 9781035853106 (Paperback)
ISBN 9781035853113 (Hardback)
ISBN 9781035853137 (ePub e-book)
ISBN 9781035853120 (Audiobook)

www.austinmacauley.com

First Published 2024
Austin Macauley Publishers Ltd®
1 Canada Square
Canary Wharf
London
E14 5AA

Thank you to my editor, Benedicta Norell, for all you taught me, which was invaluable.

Thanks to my late and inspiring friend and colleague, Marilyn Imrie, who, along with Abby Aron, Maria Aitken, and Sylvestra Le Touzel, encouraged me to tell this story.

Many thanks to my sister, Pauline Owen, whose proof-reading skills are second to none.

Thank you to Sally Carpenter and Caroline Holdaway for always being there for me.

Thank you, Georgia Pritchett, for changing my life for the better.

Finally, thank you to my two boys, who will probably never read it, but this book is for you.

And for all those treasure hunters who dream of what may lie under the ocean.

A WORLD WAR II LIBERTY SHIP

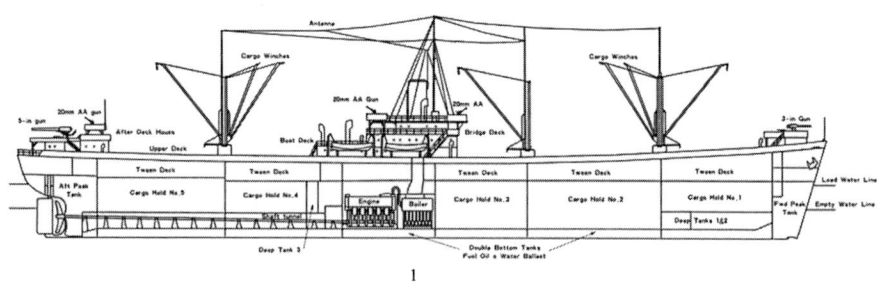

---

[1]Kallgan (https://commons.wikimedia.org/wiki/File:Libertyship_linedrawing_en.jpg)

Chapter One
1944

It was stifling in the engine room as the wiper checked the two oil-fired boilers for the third time that morning. The air was thick and oppressive, and he dabbed his greasy brow with a rag. They had just left Jamaica and were chugging their way through a heavy, sparkling blue Caribbean Sea on board the U.S. Liberty ship, the SS *John Barry*. Not that the crew had been allowed ashore there. Below decks, their around-the-clock duties had remained the same.

The third assistant shouted down above the persistent din of the pistons that battered the ears.

"Grab your helmet. Drill on deck in five!"

The sunlight pierced the wiper's eyes when he emerged through the hatch, the unrelenting grinding of metal still thrashing inside his head. He squinted his way to an assembly of familiar faces. At his station were an assortment of ranks: a signalman, two gunners, the second mate and ordinary seaman and one able, an oiler from his department and then the baker and a galleyman from the mess. They went through the drill routine as they had done countless times before.

"Have you heard?" said the second. "We're changing course. New York."

There was a murmur of approval at the prospect of some depravity in the bars and dives of the city. At the signal, they returned to work, dreaming of a night in the town. But on arriving in New York, before any of the crew could disembark, the ship slipped silently from her mooring and continued on her way to Philadelphia to carry out a special secret mission.

The speed at which Liberty ships could be constructed had allowed the United States of America to mass-produce cargo ships faster than German U-boats could sink them. By 1943, three Liberty ships were being completed daily, mostly by a female work force. These ships were designed to keep the flow of much-needed cargo moving from the U.S. to Russia and Britain. They were named after distinguished Americans, manned by members of the U.S. Merchant Marine and carried very limited firepower. Many were lost before arriving at their destinations. One of these was the SS *John Barry*.

In 1943, the U.S. Joint Chiefs of Staff considered the world oil situation and concluded that the Allies could soon run out of oil. The California Arabian Standard Oil Company agreed to undertake a secret project as long as the U.S. government would help fund the initiative. This secret only came to light when related correspondence was declassified many years later.

The project was the construction of a massive oil refinery in Saudi Arabia. The work force at the time included Sunni Muslims who strictly observed the religious laws of the Koran, one of which is that goods and services can only be exchanged for goods and services of equal worth, making paper money unacceptable. As part of its lend-lease programme, the United States agreed to provide silver ryals as payment and, unusually, to mint them as well. In order that they were acceptable to the Sunnis, the inscription on the coins stated that they were struck in Saudi Arabia, even though they were actually minted in Philadelphia.

A ship was now needed to carry the silver coins from the U.S. to Saudi Arabia.

Up on the bridge of the SS *John Barry*, the captain, John Ellerwald, had received an unexpected radio signal to divert to New York and then onto a secret location where he was to pick up a cargo that he was not expecting to carry, nor would he know its destination until they were once more at sea.

In Philadelphia, the crew waited and wondered while their ship was fitted out with a timber-built strongroom. When they saw guards with machine guns on board, even the purser commented on the high level of security.

"Very, very unusual," he whispered. "But not for us to know," he added when he saw a question forming on the lips of the bosun.

As much as the crew speculated as to what was being loaded under the cover of darkness, none of them knew anything other than this was a very exclusive consignment. In fact, thirty-seven tonnes of silver ryals had been packed into sacks and then into boxes. A thousand coins in each sack and two sacks per box. Seven hundred and fifty boxes were then lowered into the strongroom, but there was nothing in the manifest to say where the strongroom was.

And what of the other containers packed into the lower holds but not listed in the ship's manifesto? What were in those? In sworn statements given to investigating officers of wartime losses, it stated that, apart from 65 tonnes of trucks, 108 tonnes of cranes, 11 tonnes of auto parts, 23 tonnes of earthmoving equipment and large quantities of steel plate and piping, the SS *John Barry* also carried a very special cargo of 3 million silver ryals and an amazing $26 million worth of silver bullion, worth about $380 million by the late 1980s.

This claim was repeated in March 1945 in a report given to the US Coast Guard in Washington, DC. No record has yet been found to substantiate the additional silver required to make up the reported bullion on board the SS *John Barry*.

However, the silver bullion not appearing on the ship's manifest is not necessarily significant, as its exclusion means nothing under wartime conditions. Many secret cargoes were never directly manifested, and there is also an amazing paper trail of 90,000,000 ounces of silver bullion that ends in New York. In 1944, the US signed an agreement underwritten by the UK government with India for the lend-lease of 100,000,000 ounces of silver. On 10 June, a requisition form was raised by the British Ministry of Supply for 90,000,000 ounces of silver in bar form for transfer to the government of India. On 19 June 1944, the US Treasury Department authorised the transfer. On 29 June, the SS *John Barry* berthed in New York. There was an unverified rumour that trucks bearing an unspecified cargo loaded her at night before she left New York for Philadelphia on 4 July. The ship was carrying approximately 930 tonnes less than her full load. In wartime conditions, it is unlikely that she would have sailed short of capacity. It was also noticeable to an outsider that there were a significant amount of military vehicles on view; it was unusual to see so many airplanes, tanks and locomotives lashed to the top deck. But unlike the silver ryals, there is no absolute proof that the silver bullion was also on board. It is this unsolved mystery that makes the SS *John Barry* one of history's most intriguing treasure ships.

Joining a convoy, the SS *John Barry* arrived in Port Said, Egypt on 18 August 1944. From there, it was under orders to sail on to Saudi Arabia without an escort. For ten days, the ship maintained a tense blackout and radio silence as it zigzagged across the Indian Ocean in an attempt to avoid detection from German submarines, but the SS *John Barry* was already under close observation.

Patrolling off the south coast of Oman, a German U-boat, the U-859, had picked up the sound of the Liberty ship's engines. The captain, Johann Jebsen, set his sights on a lone merchant vessel clearly visible on a moonlit night. His first torpedo missed, but the second tore open her hull. By the time the third torpedo struck, the crew of sixty-eight had clambered into lifeboats and were being tossed around in the swell. One of the lifeboats capsized, and the sliced-open ship broke in half. The bow plunged downwards into the depths of the ocean and was gone.

The wiper looked around his lifeboat at the assembled group. Drenched but alive, their faces lit up with horror as they stared at the fires on board their recent home. The acrid smell of burning diesel filled the night sky. There had been no time to reach for a helmet or a life jacket; they were now men, not marines, watching in disbelief as the stern of the SS *John Barry* rose up out of the water and hung silhouetted against the moon before slowly submerging under a whirlpool of air where there had once been a ship.

Commander Johann Jebsen lowered his periscope and turned calmly to his log, where he entered his success. Three days later, he made another entry, a direct hit on a British merchant ship, the SS *Troilus*. Twenty-two days later, in the Malacca Straits and as a result of Enigma intelligence information, the British submarine *HMS Trenchant* intercepted his U-boat, which sank immediately, drowning forty-seven men, including Commander Jebsen.

In his 1972 book, *Liberty Ships: The Ugly Ducklings of World War II*, John Gorley Bunker writes, "The SS *John Barry* [is] a most unlikely treasure ship…securely crated and locked in her holds is a fortune more fabulous than even Ali Baba and his forty thieves could have hoped for…"

Chapter Two
January 1994

"The little bit (two inches wide) of ivory on which I work with so fine a brush" is how Jane Austen described her writing. She was a miniaturist who did not live to see her books reach across the globe, entertaining people from different cultures with her wit and her vision and speaking volumes to anyone who has ever fallen in love. Performing extracts from her novels, Geraldine had created a hugely successful show that the British Council had been only too pleased to promote in as many countries where they had a presence as could be fitted into one long tour. But a one-woman show can be a very lonely affair, and Geraldine asked me if I would go with her. The exotic locations on offer were too good to turn down. It could not help being an adventure, but like all adventures, it was not altogether the one I was expecting.

I was summoned to the headquarters of the British Council in London and handed a fistful of air tickets and an itinerary. Most of the destinations did not connect geographically but were in date order, depending on who could have us when. European cities were followed by Israel, America, India, Sri Lanka, Pakistan and even the Maldives Islands. I arranged the travel, managed the production, lit the show if there were lights to light it with, sometimes putting red wires into live sockets if there were no plugs. This once led to me setting fire to the lighting board, but Geraldine continued with her performance in spite of the smoke coming from the corner of the stage. We prided ourselves on our professionalism. Together, we attended every reception in every city where we played.

Wearily, we returned to the UK and performed the show sporadically, mainly on a Sunday evening at a not very warm or welcoming venue. We were given a sparse dressing room, complete with sandwiches that had usually been in there for some time, and we listened to the chatter of the audience over the tannoy as they slowly filled the auditorium. On the stage was some make-shift furniture provided by a reluctant technician who had given up his Sunday for some overtime and, like us, wished he was at home.

We had already decided that our little show was nearing its natural conclusion, and one winter's night at a particularly shabby location in Swindon, we talked about this being our last. We packed up our props and costumes before dutifully turning up to the after-show reception to make the obligatory polite conversation. We were quite lightheaded, almost giggly at the prospect of bringing our little entertainment to an end, until we found ourselves unexpectedly cornered by a portly gentleman with plucked eyebrows and a surprising smattering of make-up.

"We are so honoured by your presence here at our unassuming thespian establishment, Miss McEwan. Allow me, if you will, to introduce myself. I have the fortunate position of being the press secretary for His Royal Highness Sheikh Ahmed Farid al Aulaqi, formerly a prince from Yemen now living in the Sultanate of Oman."

His name was Henry, and we listened politely as he went on to tell us he had previously been press secretary to all kinds of important heads of state. We had never heard of any of them.

"You must come to Muscat and perform your Jane Austen show there. It is still a closed country, but I can pull some strings; you would be guests of the sultan and will be well looked after. I can assure you of that."

"I'm not really performing it abroad anymore," Geraldine said with a smile that was intended as a no.

"Oh, but you must," insisted Henry. "You will not regret being a guest of His Royal Highness."

We were both amused and bewildered by this sudden invitation. We rather liked him.

"A real-life Mr Collins," Geraldine mused, referring to a character she had just portrayed in her show.

For several months after we met, Henry persisted with this invitation. Many faxes followed, and when he learned I was in the process of trying to set up my own TV production company, he became excited at the prospect and promised me meetings with investors if we would come to Oman. *Why does he want to help me?* He told me there was an exciting new film project on the horizon that could be of great interest, very top secret; all would be revealed in good time.

Geraldine, keen to support any breakthrough that would help my new company become established, agreed to perform in Muscat, the capital of Oman. And before long, we found ourselves boarding a plane at Heathrow. We were re-routed around war-torn Iraq and over the vast expanse of Saudi Arabia, dots of fire from its oilwells lighting the night sky. We changed planes in Dubai, taking a smaller one across the Arabian Peninsula, where we landed at Seeb Airport. Henry was waiting to sweep us through arrivals with *special papers* that were scrutinised and stamped by officials. Oman was not, at this time, open to tourists, but, as we were soon to discover, invited foreign nationals do not always make the best guests either. Henry, clearly overexcited by Geraldine's arrival, drove us erratically around the city, talking all the way, his large frame squashed into the driver's seat of a car far too small for him. The air conditioning was on full blast, accompanied by the call to prayer on the car radio. Henry bellowed above the noise, taking his hands off the steering wheel to gesticulate.

"See the gorgeous flowers adorning the roundabouts and along the highway in hanging baskets. His Royal Highness personally supervises all of this. He is driven around at night to approve the look of them. He loves flowers."

It was true Sultan Qaboos had given orders that the city should be aesthetically pleasing. Flowers growing in a desert is a sign of affluence, of success.

The Sultanate of Oman is the Switzerland of the Middle East, known for its diplomacy and peace-making deals largely due to the fact that it follows the Ibadi strain of Islam rather than Sunni or Shia, which makes it well-placed to act as a broker in hidden exchanges behind closed doors. With a coastline more extensive than the whole of Italy, it is a sea-faring nation with an extended maritime history. It hangs below the modernised United Arab Emirates and is flanked by Saudi Arabia to the west and the Republic of Yemen to the south. A large part of it consists of the Empty Quarter, an area where temperatures rise above 50 degrees Celsius.

We checked into the Intercontinental Hotel, the only large hotel in Muscat at the time, apart from the opulent Al-Bustan, and it was run by an Englishman. Our audience was primarily made up of expats who had settled in Oman and a few bemused Omani officials. Although they were very appreciative, we were left wondering what they made of it and why they were there in the first place. And come to that, why were we there as well? There was an abundance of social, but bemusing, events organised solely for us. Word had clearly spread that there was a distinguished British actress in town.

A typical day was spent lunching with a munitions dealer or conversing at a supper party with an old army colonel who had arrived in Oman as a mercenary and had never left. There had been a population increase in recent years, or as one expat, a doctor no less, so eloquently remarked, "They are breeding like rabbits, and they've stopped dying like flies." I wondered what other gems of wisdom he delivered to his patients. Oman had spent wisely on its people, unlike some of its neighbours, despite producing more sludge than refined oil and thought to be the poor relation in the Middle East. Medicine, hospitals and health care were all part of the sultan's policy as well as an education for all. Ninety percent of the children of both sexes could now read and write.

Geraldine and I found solace in laughing at the surreal situation we found ourselves in. This had all come about from one conversation in a theatre bar. On one occasion, we stood on the veranda of the British Embassy, an old colonial building with heavy white shutters and fans, while the Indian servants, wearing white gloves and little white hats perched on top of their heads, flitted silently around, attending to our every need. I gazed out over the original Muscat, once flanked by two forts. The old part of the city was being torn down to make way for the new.

"It's a shame to see it go," the ambassador lamented. "This lovely building too is soon to be demolished."

"But why?" I asked.

"For an Omani, new is good. New is wealth and prosperity. Ostentatious is even better."

He sighed and sipped his martini. "Jan Morris would no longer recognise the country she wrote about when she was still called James."

"And the sultan, does he approve of all this?"

"He wants what his people want. He genuinely wants the best for his people. But he bloody loves England, you know, thinks of it as his second home."

As a teenager, Sultan Qaboos was sent to be privately educated by a couple in the Suffolk countryside, where he loved wandering around near Bury St Edmunds. He trained at Sandhurst and was a diligent soldier who went on to serve as an officer in a British regiment. He also worked for a while at Hertfordshire County Council, learning about local government. On returning to Oman in 1966, he was placed under virtual house arrest in his father's palace in

Salalah because the then sultan did not like his son's modern approach to governing. Before 1970, life in Oman was firmly rooted in the Middle Ages. Under the repressive rule of the old sultan, nobody was allowed to leave Oman or travel anywhere without permission from him. Tribal warfare was still an accepted part of life and so was slavery. People were not allowed to smoke, wear glasses or use western medicines.

Qaboos planned to overthrow his father with the support of the British Government, with the aim of ending his country's isolation and using oil revenues to modernise it. The coup was successful, and he acceded to the throne in 1970. One of the first things he did was abolish slavery.

Not only did the sultan care about the flowers on his roundabouts, but his passion for music was something which he wanted everyone to share. By decree, classical music played every morning on the one and only radio station, sometimes blaring out of loud speakers by the roadside. Sultan Qaboos believed that music was good for his people.

"He once flew the London Symphony orchestra out to play for him and, as he had kept them waiting for an hour and a half, to make amends he gave each member of the orchestra a gold watch and supplied a feast for the whole audience." The ambassador found this highly amusing.

I looked to see if he too was wearing a gold watch, and I thought about my new and, so far, bogus production company having not yet produced anything. *Is this how it works? They fly you out to perform?*

The ambassador continued, "He revisits England whenever he can, you know. In Blackpool, he once heard a barrel organist playing. He was so intrigued by the sound that he paid for the organist, his wife and the barrel organ to be transferred here so they could teach him how to play. They were extremely well paid but missed their old life, so they relinquished their wealth and returned to Blackpool."

To this day, the barrel organ remains un-played in the palace.

Chapter Three

After our performances had come to an end, Henry invited me to stay on in Muscat. He was lining up some *introductions* and insisted that it was in the best interests of my newly formed company to come to these meetings.

"And there will be one very important meeting about the *top-secret* project," he added mysteriously. Geraldine and I were intrigued, but it was never the plan not to return to England together, even though she was returning to her family and I was not. But my empty office seemed even less enticing now that there was a top secret on offer. I was hungry to know more. And so I decided to stay.

We escaped to the beach to watch the sea fold the sun under a glass sheet and shatter into a shower of orange shards stretching towards us. The air was pungent with the aroma of burning frankincense from home-built fires. It was the coolest part of the day and popular with the locals. Men sat on their haunches and shared a hookah pipe. Children played and waved at us; whole families promenaded on the sand. Women chattered to each other as they followed their husbands, who went ahead holding each other's hands.

Our long journey together was at an end. We had come to look over the Gulf of Oman before Geraldine returned to London. Before we parted, she pressed an inscribed copy of Jane Austen's *Persuasion* into my hand. We both understood that going our separate ways would be strange. Geraldine was to return to the National Theatre, where once again she would be in the company of other actors and in a world that was familiar to both of us. There was nothing familiar about where I was heading. The parting was a painful one.

After she had returned to England, there was a palpable shift in the hospitable climate. Suddenly alone, I was no longer travelling with a highly regarded famous actress, and, consequently, I was no longer a guest of the Intercontinental Hotel. I had to relocate to Henry's apartment in the Ruwi Valley, where the old airstrip used to be.

Henry came to collect me, and, as we were driving there, I asked him about the investors for my company he had alluded to.

"Ah," he said with a grin, "the way things are done in Arabia is very different from Blighty. You cannot call meetings; you have to wait for them to summon you."

"And how long does that usually take?"

"Depends, can be very sudden or can take a year."

"A year?" Waiting in a Middle Eastern country for a year did not seem like an attractive option. *What about my flat, my life and my plans waiting for me in London?*

"All will become clear in time. After all, you are the chosen one who will deliver a sensational story to the world."

"Chosen one?"

"Yes, the sheikh has chosen you. This will be worldwide news."

"That's great," I said, unconvinced. "But what is this worldwide news?"

"All in good time. Here we are."

We had arrived at a concrete block of flats. As I was climbing the stairs, I realised I had very little luggage for a long stay. I would have to go to the souk and buy some clothes or at least have my own ones copied. An Indian tailor would take a pair of trousers and make up three more by the morning for very few Omani rials.

The apartment was spacious but spartan. The kitchen was devoid of any sustenance other than a copious supply of vodka and giant cans of orange juice in the fridge. Henry showed me to my room. It was entirely empty, apart from a half-pumped-up airbed. He left me to unpack.

I laid out my few clothes on the drab carpet, took out my now most treasured possession, *Persuasion*, and settled myself on the plastic sagging bed as best I could to read.

"She had been forced into prudence in her youth. She learned romance as she grew older."

The mosque right outside my window ensured that the call to prayer would never be far away. It was a sound I found soothing and reassuring as I waited for the morning and the promised meetings. I had been told to be patient; that's how things were done here. The moment would come when I would be summoned. Unfortunately, nobody could tell me when that would be or what it was about.

Henry's daily habit was to visit as many people as possible, mainly expats, some of whom had been there seemingly forever. It was a kind of sport; you would turn up, drink their gin and then weave home again along the empty roads. We went to visit the Cotterills, who boasted of having lived on the Arabian Peninsula for more than 40 years. They had seven children, all grown up and gone. She had become an alcoholic and seemed confused; her husband looked on sympathetically while she reminisced about their lives over her gin. "You remember, darling, it was the day the pope was shot?" She looked at me, trying to make sense of who I was. "He's hopeless at shopping, you know. Sent him out for an iceberg the other day, and he came back with a bloody cabbage." I admired Henry for making the effort to still go and visit them. As we got back into his toy-like car, they were hanging over the balcony on the eleventh floor. I waved as we sped off. I looked back to see two forlorn figures waving back at me.

There were many nights like these. I felt like an alien newly arrived somewhere in a past life, and I was becoming impatient. Henry loved to talk about British politics. Every day, he would thump heavily on his ancient typewriter, expressing his views and comments on the state of the UK for one of his many press releases. He was more restrained when writing about Oman, but really his favourite subject was his ideas. He especially loved *big ideas*. And currently, Henry's big idea was to raise money for my company, which he now calls *our company* so we could develop film projects together. He wanted to make a film about the orphan island states, which were still dependent on the UK, which did seem like a very good idea, especially if I could film them all. But every so often, he would hint at the REALLY big idea, presenting it as a *gift* to me for broadcasters to fight over. When pressed, he infuriatingly asserted that he *couldn't possibly give away the sultan's secrets. What is he talking about?*

On one rare evening, when I was alone in Henry's apartment, I was sitting on the floor of my room contentedly listening to the call to prayer when there was a knock at the door. I opened it to an Asian man in a suit. Outside was a black Mercedes. In the back seat was a middle-aged Englishman, his torso too long, his shoulders hunched and his head bent forward with impatience. His narrow eyes peered over a bent nose that looked like it had been broken several times. He called out from the open car window.

"Get in, we are going to the officer's mess at the Omani Tank Regiment Headquarters to meet Henry."

"Okay, well, can you give me a minute?"

"Come on. Come on. No time to lose," he barked.

I was dressed in my new Omani-style trousers and loose, long-sleeved top; he would not give me time to change into anything else. There was something about his command that was compelling and made me freeze. I did not know then that this would not be the only time I went against my will when confronted by him. I got in the car.

"Come on, put your foot down, man. Work for a change."

The driver duly shifted into drive and sped off. I squirmed and wondered if he spoke like that because the man was from India or if it was for my benefit in some distorted way. *Why am I in this car?*

"Where did you say we were going?"

"I already told you that," he snapped. "Weren't you listening?"

"Something about a tank regiment? I'm sorry I didn't catch your name. Mine is—"

"Major Gareth Johnson, Sherwood Forester. British Army."

"Should I stand to attention?" There was no sign of a uniform or a smile.

"No, no, girl. Dhofar War long over. I stayed in Oman to help out."

There was something intriguing about his inexcusable behaviour. There was a sparkle in his voice when he spoke to me, but not to his driver.

"Faster, man, don't take any notice of the speed limit!"

Helping out surely meant that he was making a tidy living serving someone important. But any more information about my captor was not forthcoming.

We arrived at a heavily armed roadblock where soldiers waved us on into an oasis surrounded by palm trees, complete with a swimming pool and a bar. Huddled around the pool were a series of one-storey wooden army huts, colonial in style, with overhead fans and verandas. Here, Major Chris Beal welcomed me.

"Ah, another Brit to join the battle. Someone bring this lady a drink," he hollered to a passing waiter. While Indian waiters attentively delivered a non-stop flow of alcohol, I saw Henry, already ensconced under a palm-leafed roof with a vodka in hand, entertaining the officers with the day's stories that he had been bashing out earlier.

The walls of the mess were decorated with portraits of previous officers and a variety of rifles from different periods. Major Beal opened an unlocked glass cabinet full of handguns and took them out one by one, as if they were newborn chicks just hatched. He fondled them lovingly while recounting their history in some detail. But what I wanted to know, like all the men I was encountering, was how he had come to be here.

"Disenchantment," he replied. "So many cutbacks in the British Army. I walked out one day and never returned. Joined an expedition across the Sahara in an airship before ending up in Oman as an officer in the sultan's army. It's a good life here."

He patted a Browning Hi-Power before putting it back into the cabinet. "You? What are you doing here?"

Before I could think of an answer, and I was struggling to think of one, he went on. "The forthcoming expedition into the Indian Ocean – is that why you're here? Are you going?"

Indian Ocean? News to me.

"Yes," I answered without conviction. *Was I?*

Cocktails were served in the mess, and I found myself standing next to an awkward Gareth towering over me like a hawk hovering over its prey. My attempts at conversation were interrupted by Henry, who, assuming that Gareth was telling me about the *secret project*, lumbered over to us.

"You know Gareth is the operational manager," he gushed, as though I would know what that meant.

Gareth interrupted him by shouting to a waiter to bring us more drinks. Looking straight at me, he said, "What kind of wine do women like?"

I waited in silence for him to answer his own question. "'I wanna go to Barbados,' they whine," he said, testing me.

An officer nearby laughed, but Henry could hardly contain himself as sweat poured onto his sparse eyebrows. He was too excited about the secret project to be diverted by jokes.

"We have been working on this for years, you know. We're going to go two miles under the sea to find the sunken treasure."

"Treasure?"

"Yes. It is going to be the biggest and most valuable treasure ever retrieved." Unleashed, words were tumbling out of his mouth so fast that foam was forming on the corner of his lips. "It will be the deepest salvage ever since the *Titanic*."

Titanic? "Didn't fifteen hundred drown on the *Titanic*?" But Henry couldn't hear me over his own voice.

"We're going to place depth charges and retrieve millions of dollars of silver coins and silver bars."

The thought of Henry travelling in a submersible more than a mile deep when he could barely fit into his car was such a ludicrous image that I began to laugh.

"We will have the full backing of the sultan with frigates and helicopters and royal launches."

"A salvage operation?" I said, still trying to process what I was hearing.

"Yes. Yes," Gareth interjected, irritated by the torrent of information spewing out from Henry and my ignorant reply. "It's been planned for some time. Where is that boy with our drinks?" He sent Henry off to find the waiter.

"So am I supposed to film from a submarine?" I enquired, trying to sound calm.

"All will be revealed in time," he grunted as the waiter hurried over to re-fill his glass. "Right. Forward into dinner."

Dinner consisted of curry followed by crème caramel, which was no sooner on my plate than Major Beal drenched it with a wine glass of Cointreau. "Blessed by the Regiment," he announced, teetering as he poured.

As the evening wore on and more alcohol was consumed, I asked Gareth if he had been part of the recent Gulf War. He said he had witnessed the horror of the Basra Road after the allied bombing but shrugged off these memories.

"You must not take life too seriously, Katie," he said, getting my name wrong not for the first time.

"It's all about logistics. Statistics show that it costs a million bullets to kill one man and that armies around the world are having to buy too much hardware to do the job." *Oh, so that's what it is about.*

"A very expensive and ineffectual way to kill someone – not at all cost-effective."

"Ah, but the British Army, being highly trained, needs nowhere near that amount," Chris Beal chimed in, wanting to be part of the war conversation.

I decided to change the subject. "Do you have a family, Gareth?"

His eyes softened and began to well. "If only I could see them more often." He said he had a young daughter back in England living in the beautiful Devon hills. *Power, money, hard to give up Arabia.*

After dinner, we retreated to the garden, where we joined the other officers for coffee and liqueurs. There was now an ugly development in the conversation as the focus switched to the Indian servants busily working around us. It was agreed that none of them were any good and that they were ruining the country.

"But they are doing all the work," I protested.

Henry leapt onto the bandwagon; only yesterday he had been extolling the virtues of Hamza, his Indian manservant, but now suddenly in his vodka induced state they were *all liars and cheats and there was not a cockroach in sight before Indians arrived in Oman*. Finally, the ranting dissipated into a wash of alcoholic fumes, and the officers went to bed, leaving a small group in a drunken inertia with one sober Indian attentively waiting should we need any more to drink.

Gareth led us to his car, where he smacked the driver's door with his baton.

"Come on. Wakey-wakey."

The driver awoke in time for some more verbal abuse before driving us back to Ruwi. It was not a comfortable ride. The theatre had sheltered me more than I had realised. And now, apparently, I was going to set sail into the unknown whether I liked the company I would keep or not.

The biggest, deepest treasure?

Henry, now deflated by the consumption of alcohol and having been admonished for already having said too much, could not be drawn further on the matter. That is until he was back at his apartment, having one final nightcap, when he blurted out:

"It is an American Liberty ship, the SS *John Barry*. Full of silver bullion and coins, and oh, by the way," he called out over his shoulder as he tottered off to bed, "Sheikh Ahmed says he will invest in our company."

Chapter Four

This production company, which somehow I now shared, was still so new. Barely begun. Only a few months ago, while lying on a trolley, pushing myself around under the shallow Hampstead Theatre stage searching for a leak in a tank of water that was part of a set design, I began to wonder if it was time for a career change. A large drip of stagnant water stung my eye. *Yes, it was.*

The next question was how. Perhaps I could take what I had learned in the theatre and use it to explore a new medium, that of film and television. Part of the attraction was that, having spent my entire adult life working in the theatre at night, I had never actually watched any TV. Their secrets were waiting to be explored. If only I could find a way in. I was shivering at the brazenness of my idea when the designer called out to me.

"Have you found it? The water level is still going down."

Bloody stupid idea to have a tank on stage in the first place. The poor actor having to immerse herself in cold water every night coated with green slime. She was not the only one immersed in green slime, and there was only one thing for it: I would crawl free and become a famous producer.

A party was given, presents, speeches. My new life. My new venture *sure to be a great success*. Lots of speeches. I stood at the top of the stairs and thanked them all. Out of the corner of my eye, I spied my successor, not quite in the swing, wishing me luck for this new and glittering career I had announced for myself. Except it wasn't glittering. Gone was the glamour of west-end opening nights and working with the greats. Precious moments with writers and actors. Arthur Miller, David Mamet, Harold Pinter. I was always asking them to talk to me. I thought they held the key to the universe, that they could provide some answers. If Jane Austen had been alive, I would have been straight down to Hampshire to visit her. While rehearsing Tennessee Williams's play, starring Lauren Bacall, I had dared to invite Harold to go for a walk with me. We sat in deckchairs opposite each other in Green Park. No sooner had I started to speak than I felt foolish and confused. I wanted to have some sort of intellectual conversation with him about love and the world, but instead I sat folded into an unnatural shape in my chair and stared at him. He told me he was meeting his wife Antonia Fraser later and the thought of seeing her was exciting to him. I was so surprised to learn that such feelings could exist within a marriage that when he left, I sat for a long while, longing for romance.

A few years later, I met with Harold again when I was the production manager at Hampstead Theatre. It was my first production there, and again, Harold was directing. He had attracted Faye Dunaway to the tiny hut in Swiss Cottage, quite a coup, but they soon made themselves unpopular with the backstage staff, demanding chilled white wine and Caesar salad with a little bit of Dijon mustard on the side. For a crew that lived off pizza and bacon sandwiches, fringe and film stars never really mixed. Our little team worked hard to put on a new play every eight weeks. We hardly ever went home. For six years, the busy backstage life of an underfunded theatre became my family. And I was never alone for a moment.

Now in my empty office with no ringing telephones, the silence was tormenting.

Where to start?

I bought a laptop and attended film school, albeit only a short course. I had some business cards printed with the word *Producer* under my name, even though I had yet to produce anything. I wrote proposals of my ideas over and over and sent them off to broadcasters, who sometimes replied, often not. Occasionally, there was a sniff of interest, a moment of hope, swiftly followed by rejection. I was already running out of money, and the rent was due. My love life was complicated and shrouded in secrecy. My part-time partner took privacy to an extreme. No shouting from the rooftops for us. And now here I was, wide awake on my half-deflated airbed, with the sun already rising over the mountains to the sound of the morning call to prayer. And no return date. Meanwhile, a team of steadfast treasure hunters was coming together for the final stages of the grand project they had been working on for years.

Sultan Qaboos's chief advisor was Brigadier Sir Timothy Landon, who had been at Sandhurst with him. Aware of the wreck's location in Omani waters, Landon was keen to find an answer as to how to retrieve the SS *John Barry's* valuable cargo. Would-be salvagers had approached the U.S. government from time to time, but due to the wreck's position at such extreme depths, the salvage was deemed impossible. The big motivator to go deeper into the oceans was the success of finding the *RMS Titanic* in 1985. With the advancement of new technologies, Bob Ballard, the celebrated oceanographer, proved it could be done. The pictures and personal belongings salvaged at such enormous depths were exhibited all over the world and captured the imagination of all treasure hunters. If they could reach that one, then why not others?

In Sussex, an ex-marine, Rob Hudson, replaced the phone receiver and smiled. He had just achieved the result he was hoping for. His attention had been drawn to the SS *John Barry* by a close friend, whose name, coincidentally, was also John Barry. So when Hudson discovered that the wreck was close to Oman, a country in which he had an affinity for he had both lived and fought there, he wondered if perhaps the hand of fate was leading him towards the lost treasure.

He undertook some extensive research by visiting the vaults of the National Maritime Library in Washington, DC. He was satisfied that the silver coins had been loaded onto the SS *John Barry* before sailing from Philadelphia in 1944. He suspected that the strongroom would be in the bowels of the ship in Hold 2, as the other holds were more accounted for. Rob was a measured man who needed facts, and there was no doubt in his mind that the silver coins were there, ready to be retrieved. He had found no evidence of silver bullion, but he beamed at the thought of such a bonus should they find it.

He telephoned the baton-waving Gareth, whom he had fought alongside during the Dhofar War in southern Oman. By now, Gareth was a prominent businessman in Muscat who had built up a conglomerate involving oil field support, shipping and hotels on a large scale. He owned the biggest privately owned trucking haulage company in the Middle East. He also partnered with the enigmatic and exiled Sheikh Ahmed Farid in several business ventures, which included some undercover activities to restore the Sheikh family's fortunes back in Yemen. But he had not forgotten his comrade in arms and remembered the young commando with the spiky blond hair and the strong sense of authority.

"How goes it, Hudson? Still alive, then?"

"Very much so. I'm looking for someone rich to invest in a money-making project."

"Isn't everyone?"

"Yes, but not often does it involve millions of dollars in your own backyard or, in this case, the sultan's backwaters." Rob knew he had Gareth hooked. "We're talking treasure, Gareth. Lots of it."

Before long, Rob, Gareth and Sheikh Ahmed Farid were meeting in a London hotel, and the Ocean Group was born. Tim Landon was understandably intrigued to hear that the treasure belonged to Oman when Sheikh Ahmed approached him with a plan to retrieve the wreck. The Ocean Group was given the full backing of the royal household.

Rob Hudson became the project manager for the Ocean Group and the leader of the salvage expedition. Apart from having a personal history in Oman, he was also extremely experienced in the offshore oil industry. He knew that holding a recovery vessel in position for long periods against the wind and high seas was going to be a massive challenge. But now he could access huge sums of money.

At such depths, he needed a 'DP' vessel, a ship with a computer-controlled Dynamic Positioning system. By operating the right combination of propellers and thrusters, the computer should hold the ship in its correct position. But this vessel had to be capable of lowering a large, heavy contraption through a moon pool, literally a hole through the middle of the ship, to minimise movement in poor conditions. In place of a drill bit on the end of the *string*, which consisted of a 100 tonnes of pipe each section manually screwed together, a device would have to be invented that was powerful enough to smash through steel decks a mile and a half below, scoop up the silver and return to the surface, all by remote control. Instead of rotating, the drill would have to be converted into a 'grab" to open and close and lift like those frustrating grabs in fairgrounds that never yield the fluffy toy you have set your heart on. Only this grab would weigh 50 tonnes and be capable of exerting over 400 tonnes of pulling power from the drill pipe. No such technology existed. But first, Hudson had to find a ship used by oil companies that could drill at very deep levels.

A French underwater cable-laying company, TravOcean, owned just such a drill ship, so the Ocean Group chartered and subsequently bought the *Flex LD* from them and hired its crew. Rob Hudson then approached another French company, Ifremer, the obvious choice to create, build and operate the grab system. They also provided Jean Roux, a former submarine commander with the French Navy, to act as salvage master. A tall, wiry man with a serious demeanour, unlike his counterpart, the friendly Pierre Valdy, who was short and sturdy and constantly smiling. Pierre was a brilliant engineer who had explored the wreck site in a submersible during the survey. He was full of enthusiasm for the project and responsible for designing the 50-tonne, video-equipped grab.

For several years, the actual concept of using a grab from a drill ship for deep-sea salvage had been proposed by various forerunners. It had probably originated from the recovery of a large section of a Russian submarine found in very deep waters off Hawaii during the Cold War in the 1970s, a top-secret operation known as Project Azorian and the most expensive ever funded by the CIA.

Jane Austen had brought me to the edge of a whole new era in shipwreck technology. Fully equipped, the *Flex LD* was due to set sail from Singapore in October that year. Sheikh Ahmed wanted everyone to know about this remarkable treasure hunt that would centre the world's attention on Oman. Not only had he awarded the film rights to me but I now had the opportunity to launch my company with a sensational story. It was dawning on me that this was not some trip on a boat or a dive off the side. This was going to be a major operation. *And I was part of it.*

Chapter Five

My mission was clear: return to London, where I would obtain a commission from a broadcaster, put a film crew together, pick up the salvage ship in Singapore and sail to the site of the mystery treasure. Simple.

My deserted office seemed a little more tolerable now that I was about to produce my first film. The irrational decision I had originally made under the stage suddenly seemed not so bad a move after all. I had my outstanding proposal; all I had to do was decide which television network would have the privilege of broadcasting it, depending on who bid the most money for the film rights, and I would have lift off.

Unfortunately, the networks did not seem to share my enthusiasm for treasure hunting. But I still had my story, and it was a good one. Moreover, it was all mine. Or so I thought. But there was a twist that was about to show up at my front door in the form of two of the most unlikely American individuals.

"Here, have a peanut," said the silver-haired bear of a man standing on my doorstep alongside a short, wiry man, who quietly smiled as the bear handed me a pair of peanuts in its shell. There had never been any mention of any American interest in the wreck while I was in Oman, but now these two men had arrived at my little attic flat, claiming that the SS *John Barry* was theirs.

"We heard that you're the official filmmaker for the expedition," he continued, "and seeing that we were passing through London on our way to the salvage ship, we decided to pay you a visit."

My curiosity was aroused, and I felt compelled to make no objection. Soon they were supping beers at my kitchen table, and we talked late into the night.

Jay Fiondella had a rugged white beard to match his hair, chiselled good looks and the swagger of a man who knew how to take care of himself. Brian Shoemaker was the opposite of Jay. He was small and thin and thoughtful.

"We met through the Explorers Club. When we're through with this caper, we'll make damn sure you become a member," Brian assured me.

"Oh, I'm just a filmmaker," I lied, as I was not going to tell them that I had never made one.

"You'll be more than that by the time we're done. Here have another peanut," said Jay.

"What's with the peanuts?"

Brian laughed. "I guess your fame doesn't reach this far, Jay. Frank Sinatra nicknamed him *Peanuts* Fiondella."

"I was a friend of the astronaut, Alan Sheppard, who presented me with the Astronut," added Jay, grinning with pride.

"An Astro-nut?"

"Yes. A Chez Jay peanut. I had given him to take to the moon and back, which he duly did as commander of Apollo 14. I kept this famous nut behind the bar until the actor Steve McQueen tossed it into his mouth and was about to eat it…"

"From then on, it was kept in a deposit safe," Brian continued the story. "Jay owns Chez Jay's, the greatest dive in Santa Monica. He loves to serve gourmet peanuts to his customers, don't you, Jay? The floor is littered with peanut shells that crunch beneath famous feet." Jay beamed, enjoying hearing about his famous bar.

"So, you're Californian, then?" I asked him.

"Nah, originally from the East Coast, but one glimpse of Hollywood and I decided to move there."

Jay's good looks had helped cast him in some TV Westerns, but he was not content with bit parts. He had also run a hot air balloon company, which drew attention to him and was handy for promoting the tiny restaurant in Santa Monica that he had bought for very little money. He then set about making it a popular dive bar for Hollywood stars, and this brought him the fame he had been yearning for. His secret was to have a back room that was completely private and a policy of never talking about his customers to anyone, especially the gossip icons who menacingly roamed Los Angeles at that time. He banned cameras and autograph seekers, and word soon spread that the stars were safe at Chez Jay's.

"That's enough about you," interrupted Brian, "it's getting late. I don't suppose you could spare a bunk for the night, Cathy? London hotels are very expensive."

I realised that was their objective all along, but I didn't really mind. They were intriguing company. Jay reached into his pocket, and I thought I was about to receive another gourmet peanut, but instead he took out a few pieces of porcelain, blue and white fragments discovered on a 17th-century shipwreck in the China Sea. He pressed them into my hand.

"Here, in exchange for our board and lodging."

Brian was also appreciative of my hospitality. He was courteous and precise when imparting information. A wry smile would turn into a glance in my direction when Jay was talking, but he did not contradict him; he listened carefully, occasionally interjecting with a fact or two as he regaled me with stories of how the two met and how they came to be here.

The two of them had nothing in common except a love of adventure and the thrill of the chase. Jay was a dreamer, Brian a pragmatist. Their backgrounds could not have been more different. Jay had never really known who he was, so he invented himself and then set out to live life to the full, whereas Brian was a military man through and through. He had flown helicopters in support of the United States Antarctic Research Program and had a master's degree in oceanography. After a career in the U.S. Navy, he became the commanding officer of the Naval Arctic Research Laboratory, and later, he was appointed commander of the Naval Support Force in Antarctica.

"Ice Station Zebra!" Jay exclaimed. But Brian simply smiled and added no further comment.

Jay had always loved mystery stories. He loved to solve them. He would read up on the disappearance of ships and missing aircraft, and he would set about making them part of his personal history. Throughout his life, Jay was on the lookout for adventure, and he would mount exciting expeditions, which he never had the resources to complete. He had to rely on others to do that for him, but somehow he always managed to be involved in some capacity, even if those around him did not quite know what that capacity was. He craved the romance of solving a mystery, whether it was to be found at sea or under the ice, as when he went in search of *The Lost Squadron*, six American P-38 fighter planes and two B-17 bombers that had disappeared under a remote icecap in Greenland.

"That's where I came in," Brian said. "Jay was in California. I was in Oregon. Jay was looking for an expert on polar exploration. I helped him with the research."

Jay spent three years investigating, but his money ran out, and he had to abandon the project. Within five years, an unrelated search team found the planes precisely 250 feet below the frozen spot where Jay had left his markers.

Another one of Jay's ventures that spectacularly backfired was his long-term dream to build a Spanish galleon in his backyard. Over the course of twenty years, he painstakingly put together a replica with a luxurious interior to go with his playboy persona. The galleon frequently changed names depending on who was his current girlfriend at the time. Finally completed, he had the ship trucked to the local shipyard. En route, it broke in two and fell onto a narrow slip road blocking the entrance to a major L.A. freeway. Fifty thousand cars came to a standstill. Recovery vehicles tried to remove the wreckage, and eventually the authorities, under constant media pressure to restore the flow of traffic, gave up and ordered a bulldozer to smash the boat into tiny pieces. Jay, not one to miss a publicity opportunity, stood forlornly by the wreckage while the news cameras were on him and told the reporters that his dream was shattered but, "I still have my restaurant. Come visit Chez Jay's on Ocean Avenue in Santa Monica."

Undaunted, Jay looked around for something more lucrative. There were always treasure ships that could make him rich. It is so easy to skim over a life: playboy, treasure hunter, sailor, balloonist, boxing manager, part-time actor, owner of a restaurant frequented by Hollywood stars. But there was no easy way then of looking someone up. All that came across to me when Jay turned up at my flat and sat at my kitchen table that day was the impression he made in person. Just as it had been when Arthur Miller, after a rehearsal at Hampstead Theatre, had sat at that same table. There was no sneaking up on them from behind the internet; our lives were still our own.

My two new house guests had changed the dynamic of my proposal and brought a whole new story to the one I had understood while in Oman. They explained to me that wrecks with valuable cargoes are generally known about, but the problem is having the wherewithal to locate them and then the resources to retrieve them. Jay had neither, but his friend Brian Shoemaker was a meticulous researcher, and Jay, having obtained information about a wreck that was both intriguing and of historical interest, soon had him hooked. Brian went to work, spending months deep in the basements of the National Maritime Library in Washington trawling through the archives. Rob Hudson was not to know that Brian's fingerprints were all over the documents he too had been examining.

His research yielded evidence that the SS *John Barry* was not only American and carrying treasure but also that it lay at a depth that with new technology was achievable to reach. He was excited about the silver coins; they were worth enough to keep him for the rest of his days, and anything else they found was a bonus, but one thing he knew for certain was that one of the holds was loaded with tonnes of ryals and he was going to get them.

Over a period of five years, he put together a proposal in the hope that it would attract big money investors and encourage logistical partners to provide the technology to join them.

Eager for riches and exploration, Brian and Jay boldly set about the pursuit of their prize. The next level was about to lead them into a legal labyrinth that they were ill-equipped to deal with on their own. They needed assistance, and for this, they needed lawyers.

They approached Richard Malley, a lawyer who had been acting general counsel for the U.S. Navy, when Bob Ballard had needed legal advice on discovering the position of the *Titanic*. For Brian Shoemaker, Richard's Washington law firm seemed an obvious choice to secure the rights to the SS *John Barry*. But although Richard was very experienced in law, his main interest in life was himself. Intrigued by the challenge and sensing a financial reward, he welcomed the proposition. Looking around his office for a smart junior who would do all the work, he picked H. Maguire Riley, known as Mac to his friends, and together, they formed a consortium called the John Barry Four (JB4) and optioned the salvage rights to the wreck.

This information was startling to me. I had been led to believe that the wreck belonged to the Ocean Group in Oman.

"No, no," Brian protested, "once a U.S. Navy ship sinks, the ownership is transferred to the Department of Transportation, which continues to own the ship, albeit that it is lying on the bottom of the ocean. If treasure hunters are going to get anywhere with their hunt for the *John Barry* silver, they would have to present their research to the United States Maritime Administration (MARAD) and bid for the rights to salvage it."

The JB4 had visited Oman when the wreck was being surveyed, but Gareth had seen to it that they never made it onto the surveillance vessel, and so they had spent their time milling about the country and not at sea.

"But this time around, there's a signed contract clearly stating that two of the JB4 have a right to be on the salvage vessel at any one time, and we elected to go first," Jay said.

"Let's hope that at least some of the treasure will be recovered quickly"—he laughed—"before Richard and Mac arrive to replace us!"

Oh God, let's hope the film crew is there too. To miss out on the biggest story that would finally launch my company was unthinkable.

Chapter Six

The next morning, I heard the toaster, and the smell of burning reached me from the kitchen. I came downstairs to find my two guests up early, excited about continuing their journey.

"See you on board, shipmate, swag lots of swag my hearty!" Jay called out cheerily as I shepherded them both to a nearby bus stop.

"Yes, see you there," I replied with bravado, wondering how that would happen as the *Flex LD* was about to sail and I was no nearer to raising the money for a camera crew. I watched them board the bus and waved at them from a place of despair. I did not want to admit, even to myself, that I was struggling to stir up interest in the documentary with broadcasters. I was still confident that it was merely a matter of time, but I was now confused as to who really owned the wreck. There was no doubt that my two surprise visitors believed it to be theirs. I quickly revised my film proposal to include the growing cast list in this evolving story.

For Henry, spearheading the publicity campaign in Oman, not having every UK broadcaster jump at the opportunity to commission a film about this spectacular recovery could only mean I was not doing my job properly. Faxes were spewing out of the machine on a daily basis. It was inexplicable that I was not rushing back to Muscat with a full film crew. The weather window was short before the cyclone season approached, and the costs involved were immense. I needed to get a move on. He phoned frequently, and I wondered whether I should mention that I knew about the JB4. In the end, I gathered up the courage.

"I understand there will be some Americans on the salvage ship?"

"Yes, that's right. Sheikh Ahmed has been very generous in accommodating them."

"They have the rights?"

Silence.

"They are not the story. How is the film crew coming along?"

"Fine, yes," I answered. "Coming along."

Even the most sceptical, hard-nosed businessman will suddenly lose all his reason at the prospect of finding treasure, but convincing television commissioning editors that we would be successful was proving to be much harder. My carefully written documentary proposal was flung out to all the unlikely channels, as well as the obvious ones, and the answer was always the same. Could I guarantee that the treasure would be found? But guarantees are not one of the characteristics usually associated with treasure hunters. I argued that they would not have invested in a project this enormous without cause. I drew a blank. I could not persuade them.

The *Flex LD* sailed from Singapore without me.

Word came back a few weeks later that the ship was already in situ over the wreck. The whole operation was about to begin and would wait for no one. I was not going after all.

I was in my office, looking at a pile of rejected proposals, when the phone rang. It was Gareth calling from Muscat. I recognised his gruff voice immediately.

"There is a supply boat going out to the *Flex LD* in two days' time; are you coming or not?"

My heart missed a beat. Gareth went on.

"It's a working ship, need steel-tipped boots and a hard hat, none of your high heels."

As if.

All I could think was that there was no broadcaster, no film crew.

Fuck it.

"Yes," I said. "I'm coming."

Chapter Seven

I put down the phone but immediately picked it up again to ring British Airways. There was a flight to Muscat the next morning. I raced down to Camden Town High Street before the shops closed and bought a High-8 camera and some tapes. Then I went to an outdoor retailer and found some Doc Martins, which seemed particularly heavy, and a yellow hard hat. I packed very little because I could not think straight, and I was more concerned that I did not know how to work the camera. My holdall was still sitting in the hall from my last trip to Oman. I hurriedly stuffed my new possessions into it and zipped it up.

On the flight, a young, smartly dressed American was sitting in my seat and politely moved when he saw my boarding pass. I unpacked the camera and the instruction book and started to familiarise myself with them. As I read, I realised that some lights and a better microphone would have been handy. I felt amateurish and alone. But I was not about to miss out.

Arriving once more at Seeb Airport, I was met by Henry. I thought it was very thoughtful of him until I realised it was not me he was meeting. He was effusively greeting the American who had vacated my seat, whose jacket was barely creased after the long flight, his clean-cut looks enhanced by the crisp collar of his shirt.

"Welcome to Arabia, young man. I trust you had a good flight. Here, let me help you with your case. Oh, and you may have met Catherine already; she is in charge of the feature film we are making."

Feature?

The young man was Mac Riley; of course my guests had referred to him; he was one of the JB4. He turned to me and embraced me warmly, as if he had known me for years.

"No, we haven't met. Delighted that you're coming on our great adventure; we're going to have so much fun!"

"And you are one of the famous JB4?" I replied, enjoying the warmth.

"Yes, that's right, although I seem to have lost Richard." He looked around for the remaining member of the American team who had been on the same plane as us; at least Mac thought he was, but now he was nowhere to be seen.

"You must be on your way to join the *Flex LD* to meet Brian and Jay?" I went on.

"That's right. They haven't found the treasure yet, so I am excited for me—well, for us—Catherine, but sad for them as they're going to miss out."

Along with Richard, Mac was on his way to replace my two London visitors on the salvage vessel as part of their deal with the Ocean Group. For Mac, it was a much-welcome return to Oman, where, as part of the JB4, he had visited previously. These visits were not at all popular with Gareth; he resented adhering to a clause in the contract between the Ocean Group and the JB4, which meant paying for their travel and hotels when they were not actually participating in the recovery. As far as he was concerned, Rob and the Ocean Group were in charge, and he considered the JB4 merely observing as an unnecessary expense. He had made sure that when it mattered, only two of the group could be there at one time. It was a small victory on his part. But Mac saw it quite differently. He considered that the JB4 had a large stake in the enterprise and had a right to be there at all times, even if all four were not allowed on the ship together. He was already enjoying the prospect of Gareth's dismay at having to entertain them again, for he had no alternative but to give in to their demands, at least for the time being.

Mac turned to Henry. "How is my old friend Gareth? I bet he can't wait to see us."

"I'm sure he is very much looking forward to the reunion," Henry said as he shuffled off to search for Richard.

He came back without him, so we departed for the now familiar Intercontinental Hotel, assuming that Richard had somehow gone on ahead. In fact, he was still arguing with the Omani airport guards about some videos he was carrying in his baggage and had been detained. Having the other half of the JB4 squeeze into my London flat for several nights, I was curious to learn more about the other two members of the group, but I would have to wait until the following morning. I slept fitfully, anticipating our impending voyage.

Mac and I were sitting together at breakfast when an unkempt, weaselly man with an alabaster face and tousled yellow hair and, unusually for an American, uneven teeth hurried over to the buffet and started picking at the fruit. I was expecting a more powerful presence from all I had heard about him, so I was surprised at how small and shabby he looked.

"That's him," Mac said, laughing.

Richard turned and saw us and made a beeline for Mac.

"What happened? I was left stranded at the airport with no one to meet me. And now we have to leave for Salalah in a few minutes."

"The flight isn't until 4 pm," said Mac calmly, enjoying the anguish on Richard's face.

"What? But I've already checked out. What the fuck is going on?"

"And this is Catherine, by the way. She's coming with us."

Richard nodded, taking me in for the first time, but not curious enough to ask why I was accompanying them on such a unique journey.

"Nobody tells me anything," he complained.

"Henry came to meet you but couldn't find you," Mac said.

"That's because they wouldn't let me through. Thought I was carrying illicit material, the fuckwits."

At this, Richard started to stomp out of the room, but passing the buffet table again, he realised he was hungry. He piled a mountain of food onto a plate and went to sit in a corner where he could sulk silently.

"That's Richard for you," said Mac. "A brilliant lawyer, but his own worst enemy, blames everyone for everything."

"Can't wait to go to sea with him."

Mac beamed. "It will be an adventure."

Adventure. A word he was to use a lot during our time together.

Chapter Eight

On the aeroplane to Salalah in southern Oman's Dhofar Province, I observed with a little surprise a woman on board carrying a white goat. There was an array of livestock in the aisles, and men were smoking as we took off. From the window, the view was mostly desert, apart from where it fell away and stars of sunlight sparkled on a turquoise Arabian Sea. Oman's coastline is thirteen hundred miles long, but at this time, it was almost devoid of buildings. As we approached Salalah, I could make out a little cluster of dwellings huddled against the mountains. A rare sight is that the mountains in these arid parts are green. The Khareef, an annual local monsoon, habitually transforms the desert terrain into a lush, emerald landscape and even creates seasonal waterfalls. The foothills are bursting with banana plantations and date palms. It is the land of Frankincense, a reminder of its maritime history and its role in the spice and incense trade; it is the land of pirate queens and ancient capsized settlements where the Queen of Sheba once had a palace.

The verdant green slopes and the exotic smells as we descended onto the tarmac made me heady with anticipation. I was jolted back to the present by the sight of the only hotel to be seen, an incongruous concrete building hailing us with the familiar Holiday Inn sign.

That evening, we met with Commander Alan Moore, a tall good looking man with heavy jowls, dense black hair and seemingly a man of very few words. There was an air of authority about him. He represented the U.S. government's stake in the silver. He had been there for a few days and was clearly not enjoying waiting around, but, like us, he was catching the supply boat to the *Flex LD*. Dutifully, he was ready to go. The United States does not grant salvage rights without taking a percentage for itself.

Everyone is turning up for the prize.

After a day by the pool, and with Richard changing hotel rooms and generally running around trying to find information about our boat, Mac and I grew tired of the Holiday Inn and decided to hire a driver and go exploring. Even on an impromptu excursion into the interior, there was no mistaking the immaculately dressed Kentucky boy as he waltzed down the hotel stairs in his neatly creased shorts and crisp shirt. He could have been Colonel Sanders' grandson.

"Let's go and sightsee!" he called out with his mid-western drawl.

We had it in our heads that we would find the Queen of Sheba's tomb, supposedly nearby, but instead we found ourselves crossing the rock-strewn desert along an uninhabited road towards the mountains. Here, the temperature reaches over fifty degrees in the summer and is ice-cold at night. With so much wealth in Oman, the main roads were perfectly tarmacked and well-preserved as very few vehicles travelled on them. One such perfect highway stopped at a painted line across the road when we reached the nearby Yemen border.

"No go," cried Mac, "let's head for them hills!"

He pointed at the luminous green mountains that form a horseshoe around Salalah, and the driver swung around, and soon we were ascending tracks where the tarmac crumbled into dirt. A plumage of dust filled the rear-view mirror. We passed warning signs of camels crossing but saw no sign of any as we coiled our way through a thick plantation of green date palms.

"Here," said Mac, rooting in the glovebox, "take a look at this map. Where do you want to go?" I studied it for a moment.

"Arkut," I said. "It's a tiny settlement over there." I was pointing at a random name, but I wanted to have some kind of destination even if we never reached it.

As we continued on our way, it was obvious to me why Richard had chosen the man with whom I was now sharing a car. Mac's speech was sharp and articulate; every sentence he uttered was measured, as if it were being recorded on a document that could never be retracted. But every now and then, it was broken by a curl of his lip and a mischievous snigger, his eyes brightening at the absurdity of our situation. Here we were, going nowhere in particular to kill a few hours while we waited for a boat to turn up from we knew not where, which made us shiver with excitement at the prospect of an adventure at sea.

I asked him what I had been longing to know. "So Mac, how, against all the odds, did the JB4 manage to obtain the rights to the wreck and not the Ocean Group?"

I could see he was going to delight in answering me.

"Well, once the four of us had joined forces, we immediately went about organising ourselves into making a bid for the rights to salvage the SS *John Barry*. Of course, we knew that when the bidding process was advertised, there would be other interested parties, speculators and, worst of all, the sultan's representatives, Gareth and Co.; we knew we couldn't compete with them. But in fact, the bid we put in was relatively low. There were nine sealed bids, and all we could come up with was the figure of $50,000."

Mac smiled a wry smile I would soon get to know well. His eyes twinkled.

"At the last minute, we changed the bid to $50,010 in case anyone else put in a figure of $50,000, which, as it turned out, they did. Nevertheless, we were still astonished when we won."

Apparently, Richard, always in touch with the child within him, ran around his office celebrating in triumph. It was only when Mac tried to gather the money to pay the U.S. government that he discovered that none of the other three was prepared to cough up, all feigning that they did not have any cash. He alone would have to raise the funds. But the SS *John Barry's* future was now in the hands of the JB4 consortium.

"Why," I asked Mac, "had the Omani-backed Ocean Group, with all its wealth, not outbid four disparate Americans who had no idea how they were going to retrieve the wreck?"

"Good question." He chortled with a hint of triumph in his eyes. "The Ocean Group did not obtain the rights to the wreck because it did not bid for them at all."

"In fact," Mac went on, "Rob Hudson had been previously on the list of noted interest at MARAD, but when he became part of the Ocean Group, he was assured that the wreck was already theirs because of its position." [1]

It had crossed my mind on my previous visit to Oman that, if the SS *John Barry* lay one and a half miles down, this seemed very deep to be just off the coast, but apparently, the wreck belonged to the sultan, and that was not to be questioned.

---

[1] The Ocean Group had been prepared to bid more than a million dollars for the rights, but at the last minute, this was vetoed by the sultan himself, as he believed the wreck to be in Omani waters and therefore they automatically had the right to salvage the wreck.

Mac was almost laughing now. "Then we received a phone call from another American law firm that claimed to represent the Ocean Group. There was a snag, they said. After the bidding had taken place, the Ocean Group had learned that the shipwrecked SS *John Barry* lay not in Oman's territorial waters but in its economic zone."

"A snag?" I said. "I don't understand."

"A country is entitled to its natural resources within 200 miles but not to something as unnatural as 14,000 tonnes of steel belonging to the U.S. Government."

As the Ocean Group was about to find out, the United States was not about to give up its sovereign rights to one of its naval vessels, not even to a sultan. So while Richard was bouncing around his office, the lawyer representing the Ocean Group demanded that Richard sign the rights over to them.

Mac was enjoying this part of the story. "He claimed that the sultan had been promised the ship by the U.S. government, which is why he hadn't needed to bid for it. The conversation became very animated, and Richard was told, in no uncertain terms, that the Omani Navy would prevent the salvage going ahead. To which Richard replied that then they would have to answer to the U.S. 6th Fleet and hung up."

Having just declared war on Oman, the next phone call Richard received was from the secretary of state, James Baker. Baker asked him to go carefully, as the sultan really did believe he owned the wreck, and if he didn't, he felt the U.S. should give it to him. Of course, the government would protect the JB4's contractual rights, but maybe they would consider selling them to the Ocean Group? This wasn't going down very well with Richard. Baker went on to say that ultimately it was up to them, but to think about it because the US had sensitive agreements with Oman, which could be important if war were to break out in the Middle East. Richard came off the phone and was heard to say, "As if the U.S. would ever be involved in a war in the Middle East." He was resolved. No one was going to take their ship away.

Mac went to work budgeting the operation and attempting to raise the finance that would enable them to retrieve the treasure, but with $20,000 here and there from investors, he soon realised that he would need millions, not thousands. He tried to enlist a salvage company to invest, but they wanted to be paid up front to mount the operation and not take any risks. He then approached Bob Ballard of Titanic fame, but he was already working on another project.

"The scale of our undertaking started to dawn on us. It was one thing to obtain the rights, quite another to actually go about reclaiming cargo from inside a steel hold one and a half miles below sea level."

Operating in such a remote area would be both time-consuming and costly. The monsoons would dictate when any activity could go ahead, and then there was the little matter of hiring equipment that could even reach such depths. Mac soon became aware that if the JB4 was having difficulty raising $50,000, how were they ever going to raise, at the very least, $10 million? And every investor would want a return plus interest, even the U.S. The government stood to make ten percent of all cargo retrieved from the wreck.

"And do you believe the bullion is on board as well as the coins?" I asked him.

"I don't believe anything. I go by what is probable and what is possible. Just because the bullion wasn't on the manifest doesn't mean it isn't there. The U.S. Navy often substituted cargo without disclosing it."

Mac had excelled in law school and was convinced that his future resided in Washington, DC, which turned out to be true as he was soon noticed by the higher echelons of government. He would invariably achieve his objectives by careful use of diplomacy. For Mac, it was not so much the thrill of the chase but the thrill of the deal; this was what really made him know he was alive. But the deals were not going too well.

Then Richard received a fax from Sheikh Ahmed Farid congratulating him on their partnership in their pursuit of the silver and inviting them to Oman to discuss the project further.

All Mac's senses were alert; he could feel the frustration of his counterparts in Muscat, who had all the backing they needed but were desperate to save face after having embarrassingly lost *their* ship. He believed that there had to be a way of bringing the JB4 and the Ocean Group together for the benefit of all. Mac persuaded Richard to meet with them but Richard felt they would be at a disadvantage to go to Oman.

"So, he contacted a London lawyer, who agreed to organise a meeting between the two groups to take place at the Royal Thames Yacht Club in London, halfway between the U.S. and Oman. They met in the oak panelled board room there surrounded by paintings of racing yachts. They sat around a large green baize covered table. In typical Fiondella style, Jay brought unshelled peanuts to the meeting."

That sounded familiar. I couldn't help but feel fond of these Americans, who were so much easier to extract information from than Henry and Gareth.

"Ah, yes, I still have some of those shells in my flat in London."

"Then you will know that Jay never goes anywhere without them," Mac said with a wry look. "Not to be outdone, Richard brought along miniature Stars and Stripes and Omani flags and placed them around the table." Mac let out a guffaw at this image.

They sat on one side and the Ocean Group, comprising Sheikh Ahmed Farid, Gareth Johnson and Rob Hudson, on the other. Rob started by wanting to know what information Brian had unearthed in his research, and in turn, Richard wanted to know what the Ocean Group would pay for the right to salvage. Richard started with a figure of $10 million and Sheikh Ahmed with a figure of $100,000. Talks went on for two days. They got nowhere. Gareth washed his hands of the whole negotiation; as far as he was concerned, they had doubled what the JB4 paid for the salvage rights. What more did they want? Richard lost his temper, swept up all the flags from the table and stormed out, which did not go down at all well. After a moment of inertia, the rest of his party had no alternative but to follow.

"It might have ended there," Mac said wryly, "but for Brian's intervention."

Brian was sure that any chance of returning to the negotiating table had to stem from their side if they were to break the impasse, which lasted for thirty days. After having invested so much of his life in researching the SS *John Barry's* valuable cargo, he was desperate to move the venture forward, and so he took it upon himself to phone Sheikh Ahmed and say they were again ready to make a deal.

This time, the sheikh and his lawyers met with them in Washington, and they agreed, against Richard's wishes, to one and a half million dollars for the rights. While Sheikh Ahmed was on the phone in the bar buying three special edition BMWs from Germany, Richard told the other members of the JB4 that the only way he would ever sign the agreement was if they all gave him $100,000 each of their share. Mac refused, but the other two agreed, much to Mac's amazement.

Mac drew up a contract for the deal with the Ocean Group in which he stated that they wanted ten percent of any silver, coins or bullion, that was retrieved plus one hundred coins for each of them and all expenses to take the JB4 to and from the expedition.

Mac's eyes were really twinkling at me now. "We were not about to settle for anything less."

But Sheikh Ahmed's lawyers deleted the clause regarding the ten percent, and this became the next sticking point. The Ocean Group considered it was too high a risk to give them a ten percent contingency. Over the course of a week, the JB4 realised that their opponents were not going to give in. Richard now demanded another $50,000 from his JB4 colleagues if he were to agree to *not* taking ten per cent. Again, Brian and Jay agreed to this.

The deal was done.

Jay commented on the ruby-studded pen Sheikh Ahmed was using to sign the contract. "Nice pen."

Ahmed gave it to him. It is nye on impossible for an Arab prince not to give someone something once it has been admired. Mac read the agreement, signed and silently passed it over for the others to sign. They all shook hands.

"And you know what was so funny, Catherine? They had signed the wrong draft!" Sheikh Ahmed's lawyers had inadvertently printed out Mac's original draft, not the revised one.

"No one except for me had noticed! You should have seen the faces of the rest of the JB4 when I told them ten percent of the silver would be ours after all."

"But won't they realise?" I asked, astonished.

"Of course they will. Another battle in store. But they signed, and they won't want to lose face." Mac was triumphant. These were the battles he liked to win. The treasure was secondary.

The driver stopped the car and wandered off to pray, leaving Mac and I sitting in the car. He was literally snorting now at the memory. And then we became aware of the stillness in the air. It was overpowering. After so much talking, we needed to be a part of the landscape, and without another word, we decided to walk to the edge of a precipice, where we stood inhaling the scene below us.

A heat haze shimmered over the smouldering crimson-red boulders as they burned in the desert, and a distorted light radiated above the secluded town of Salalah. My breath was taken away not by the view, even though it was spectacular, but by the ear-ringing silence. The static air was warm and solid against my face, as if a breeze had never found its way to this corner of the hemisphere. When I looked at Mac, I could see he was experiencing it too—the same air that was once breathed in by the Queen of Sheba—but our thoughts were already stretching towards a faraway ocean, where we would soon be making our way to the prize.

Chapter Nine

Commander Alan Moore, or Al, as we came to know him, was in the lobby when we returned to the Holiday Inn. I wondered how long he had been standing there; you could never quite tell whether he was waiting for someone or simply waiting.

"Any news?" called Mac.

"Yes," he said.

"Yes?"

"5 am tomorrow," he informed us.

"Yippee!" Mac was excited now. "From where?"

"Mirbat," came the reply.

"And where is that?" I asked.

"It's a small fishing port. Not far from here."

If he was pleased with this information, we could not really tell, but for Mac, the whole enterprise was about to come alive. Five years since Brian's research led them to obtain the rights in 1989, here at last we were about to learn the truth of what really was loaded into the SS *John Barry* on that summer's day in 1944.

We went to the bar where I was the only woman, apart from a Swedish trio of semi-naked blonde women who were wearing what appeared to be tinfoil wrapped around strategic parts of their bodies. Crammed onto a tiny stage, they were singing Eagles songs into an over-amplified PA system. Their exaggerated thrusting dance moves made me feel uneasy as the Arab men looked on with what I detected to be a mixture of contempt and desire. Not for the first time, I felt members of my own sex were aliens to me. These were the kind of women the sailors on the *Flex LD* would be expecting when I arrived: a sexy, flirty girlie girl. What even is that – a girlie girl? *No one I recognise.* They had tried me in frocks as a child; my sister has stuffed socks in my bra to make me more *sexy* to no avail. Make-up was something to avoid, and I have not worn it to this day. I had stood looking over at the boy's playground at school and longed to join in their football game. I went home to a bedroom full of soldiers and toy cars. I was happiest when alone, where I could be myself, but as the years went on, disguise became the order of the day. Love affairs behind closed doors.

Protecting the reputation of others. It was back to the playroom, where secrets were safe. Being a woman is loaded with expectations; simply being yourself does not seem to be an option.

We were joined by Hervé, the manager for the *Flex LD* in charge of the marine crew and logistics support. He was also going to travel with us. A small, slim man with greying hair who spoke good English. He wasted no time in ordering French red wine, but after one sip, he rejected it with a wave of his hand. The heat had proved too much for it, and whisky and vodka followed, much to the Frenchman's disgust. But I was already thinking about the morning and the tiny port at sunrise, where we would join the supply boat and the long-awaited escapade would begin.

I hardly slept and was quickly down the stairs, carrying my small holdall and camera case. It was still dark as I stood in the empty hotel foyer. Hervé was next, carrying some large white picnic boxes provided by the hotel kitchen; he greeted me in French and then, seemingly unsure what to add, was silent. Commander Moore was already outside surveying the forecourt for a vehicle that would take us to the boat. Mac arrived in his newly ironed shorts. Richard was last to join us. We all scrambled into a jeep for the hour's drive to the port of Mirbat. It was here that sixteen SAS officers were killed in the 1970s during the Dhofar War. A mere six held out, killing 200 rebels, until reinforcements came.

We passed the small stronghold and gun turret, a monument to the recent past, the empty shells still lying in the sand.

Dawn was breaking as we reached the port. We clambered out of the Jeep and stared at the boat that was going to take us to the ship. I exchanged looks with Mac. A fishing dhow?

For a voyage like this? How could that be right?

"I have to say," he said, echoing my thoughts, "I was expecting a naval vessel."

The wooden dhow before us was small, old and not in a good state of repair. An image of the *African Queen* flitted through my mind, and I half expected Humphrey Bogart to be captaining it. The owner of the dhow greeted us; he was coming with us along with another Omani man with gold teeth, whom we were later to discover was our armed guard, although who he was guarding us against, we never knew. He was wearing flowing robes with the traditional tribal mussar wrapped around his head. He appeared to be twice the size of the skipper, a little, wiry man from India who was busy changing a battery. The crew consisted of the skipper's mate and one other, both Indian. He threw our luggage onto the deck, where nearby some chapatis were cooking on an open fire. There was no sign of a life raft or any lifejackets. Why was nobody saying anything? Surely someone would say something?

The boat was plainly not seaworthy; it would only be a matter of time before someone spoke out. Was I really going to be the only person who complained? *Typical woman.* I could hear Gareth's voice. *I knew you weren't up to it.* I remained silent. This was not right. I knew it wasn't right. I had promised myself that I would not go on a boat if I was in any doubt. And I had serious doubts.

Yet when the time came, it was the work of an instant. I broke my promise as I stepped on board.

Chapter Ten

There was no shelter other than the wheelhouse, a box-like structure into which two people could crawl. There was nowhere else to sit except on the open deck, which was littered with ropes and fishing nets, which were also draped over the engine. At the stern, a flimsy box frame structure hung over the side – a plank with a hole in it, which I assumed was the toilet. Apart from a smattering of English from Gold Teeth, none of the others spoke our language, so there were only a few Arabic salutations, which subsided into a lot of shuffling between us.

Mac and I positioned ourselves on the nets behind the wheelhouse. The skipper crashed into gear and reversed through a curl of blue exhaust smoke. Then, rolling cumbersomely around, we solemnly headed out of the sleepy port towards…*nowhere*.

No sooner were we at sea than Gold Teeth, or Goldie, as we now referred to him, changed into western clothes and started to chat with Hervé. All without a glance in my direction. He told him he had two wives who talked too much, although it seemed that Goldie himself had the same problem. He joked about the food on board a navy boat.

"Lunch curry and rice; dinner, rice and curry." He laughed loudly. "Me sleep at naval base. Good talking, good dinner, good bed. Go home, too much trouble with wives." He laughed some more and, in his excitement, swung the gun he was wearing above his head before throwing it onto the deck. He knelt on all fours to pray to Allah, then he lay down across the stern, taking the only shade and promptly fell asleep.

Mac was very quiet and beginning to be affected by the motion of the boat. He consumed copious amounts of Dramamine and wore a band on his wrist to ward off seasickness. Richard ridiculed the band, telling Mac what he needed were patches behind the ears, which is what he was wearing. He assured Mac they prevented the *mal de mer* as he patted his stomach vigorously.

The boat was painfully slow, working its way over the deep. I pictured some kind of underworld spiralling beneath, ready to swallow us at any moment. Richard beckoned me to come and film him presenting a U.S. Navy flag to the owner, but I chose to ignore him as I was already wondering if I had bought enough tape stock on my hurried shopping trip to Camden. Later, he took the wheel and asked me to film him driving the boat. I ignored him again. He then gave up and stood in the bow, pretending to be the figurehead, until his face suddenly turned a lime green colour, and he was violently sick over the side.

The putt-putt engine struggled against the dark purple waves as they spun up to meet us. The tiny propeller lifted out of the water and spun helplessly while the white foam beneath attempted to push us over the next crest before crunching down again. *Putt putt.* I sat beside the dhow's owner in the wheelhouse—if you could call it that—more of a plywood box that appeared never to have been finished, with its glassless window frame and missing door. Inside was noticeably bare, apart from his large body, which took up nearly all of the space, his turban brushed against the underside of the roof. Instead of a radar screen, there was a compass in a bubble that was bouncing around all over the place. Before radar was invented, you had to rely on a spyglass and a sexton, but even those were lacking. In vain, I acted out a question. "How are we going to find a ship nearly two hundred miles from the coast without radar?" My charade was received blankly as we continued to corkscrew through the swell.

Several hours later, our situation had not changed except that we were now more exposed to the burning sun. A pack of cards was produced, and I tried to play with Mac, but this only made him feel worse. Goldie sat up when he saw the cards and wanted to join in, but when I won, he promptly went back to sleep, complaining of seasickness. I picked up the Ace of Spades and decided against solitaire. At 10.30 am, there was much excitement when a ship was sighted and the owner shouted the name *Flex!* This was not very reassuring, as by anyone's calculations, the *Flex LD* was still ten hours away. There were apparently no binoculars on board, but Mac, too ill to reach for his bag, asked me to find his for him. Sure enough, the ship was an oil tanker. It was the last ship we would see.

I decided to attempt an interview with Mac. It was the first time I had taken the camera out of its case since on the aeroplane from London, and the first time I had ever filmed anything. Holding it steady was a challenge with the dhow bucking up against a wall of waves rolling beneath us and the constant spray of seawater in the air. I started by asking him how he would feel if this were to be his last day on earth, or, should I say, on the ocean. *Hilarious*.

"I feel so sick, nothing really matters, so if there is anything you want from me right now, you can have it!"

"But you are one of the few who hasn't been sick yet."

"It's willpower. I'm so glad Henry told us this would be smooth sailing because I'd hate to see it rough."

"I wouldn't fancy that either. Are you going with this swell?"

"I'm working at it. It's definitely not going with me."

"Do you think you could get to like it – become a sailor?"

"No. I keep thinking how nice it would be at home, but this is an adventure. I keep telling myself that."

He was feeling too sick to go on talking.

I flitted about the boat, asking questions that nobody could answer and clearly found irritating as they only exposed the truth. I tried Al this time, who, like me, seemed immune from seasickness.

"Have we changed course?"

"We are considerably more west than we were." He was studying the spinning compass. "I think the wind is blowing us around. The wheel is hard over."

"Has the skipper got any way of knowing how far we have come so far?"

"No."

"Have you got any idea where we are at all?"

"No, but if we keep going long enough, I think we get to England."

We were interrupted by Hervé throwing up over the side. I called to him to drink water; after all, it was the fifth time I had observed him doing this. I told Al. Al looked over at him. "Make that six."

"So you think we will see the *Flex* at around 4 pm?"

"Yes, if I knew what I was looking for. I've never even seen a picture of it."

I looked around us. "I don't think there will be many to choose from," I said. But my comment didn't raise a smile, so I went on. "It has a red hull, I believe. If we have no way of knowing how many miles we have gone and what speed we are going, how will we know if we have gone past it?"

Al thought for a moment.

"Well, basically, we're going by how many hours it's going to take. The rig should be very tall; we should be able to see it."

"I just thought there might be another way of calculating it?"

"No. I can't think of any other way; they don't have a sexton or anything to fix on to, and we don't know at what speed we are going."

"Don't boats normally know what speed they are going?"

"Usually, but then usually, they have radar and a lot of other things."

"So, eyesight, then?"

"Dead reckoning is what they call it. It's a type of navigation."

"How does that work?"

"Guesswork. I think the current is southerly, so that has to be factored in too."

"What happens when it gets dark?"

"The rig will be lit. We'll be able to pick that up."

I was aware that with our crew there was a lot of moving of clutter in order to lie down with their heads to the deck to pray, although how they knew which direction was Mecca with the compass we had was anyone's guess. Later, while looking for something to film, I noticed Richard lying on his back on the foredeck, the blistering sun burning his face. He had been seasick several times and had passed out, unnoticed by Hervé, who had his own mal de mer to deal with. Al was sitting steadfast in the kind of trance that only takes hold whenever on a boat for any length of time. Mesmerised by the distant pencil line horizon and the rhythm of the swell, my shipmates were lost unto themselves. I leaned over Richard and saw that there were blisters forming on his dehydrated lips, so I poured some water into his mouth. He swallowed. I threw a tarpaulin over him to protect him as there was no shade to be had, then I poured the rest of the water from the plastic bottle over his green face and covered it with his hat.

The waves smashed viciously against the bow, and in defiance, the dhow seemed to refuse to move forward as though treading water until somebody told it to do otherwise. It had been eight hours since we left port, and still there was no sign of the *Flex LD*. Some flying fish leapt over the bow and were gone in a flash of silver, a hint of the life teaming beneath us.

I could feel all was not well when Commander Al went to sit in front of the open window of the wheelhouse and tried to communicate with the *captain*. Without navigational equipment, there was no way of determining our speed, and Al was clearly not convinced we were on course. Hervé called out that there was no point looking for another hour and that we should be there by 6 pm, but he urged us to keep looking on all sides, which implied he also had doubts about our direction. When I questioned this, he said that we may have veered too far east, presumably to compensate for the wind and the current, but this had the effect of zigzagging, making it difficult to be sure whether we were on our bearing or not. In theory, we had to follow 80° to hit the *Flex LD,* but without knowing our speed or position and with such a dodgy compass, it was impossible to calculate.

Suddenly and without warning, Richard stood up and shouted, "This is the life!" before throwing up again and collapsing on the deck.

I left him for an hour before calling out, "Mac, have we any more bottled water with us?"

"We have three left." He gestured to the white cardboard boxes from the Holiday Inn. Inside was some fruit, a sandwich and one, only one, small bottle of Evian. The boxes were absurd, so pristine and white amongst the coiled ropes and debris on the deck. Since we had left Mirbat, there had not been any water offered to us and certainly nothing to eat. Richard was beyond either. But this posed a question. What water had we on board and what food come to that?

Stupidly, we had assumed there would be some kind of dining room on the luxury frigate that was going to transport us to our luxury yacht somewhere out there. *Water.* It was all I could think about.

As I stared at the blackening sea spluttering against the hull like a choking serpent, three sharks swam menacingly close to the rail-less deck, their fins dipping in and out, letting me know they were there.

"What are you waiting for?" I called to them.

I checked Richard was still breathing so as not to waste the last drops from the plastic Evian bottle. *Evian.*

I had once visited Evian in Switzerland on one of those soul-searching trips when travel was thought to bring answers, even though I didn't yet know the questions. Money was scarce, so I could not travel very far. I sat miserably in a formally starched dining room at my separate table and drank brandy. The next day, in the spirit of adventure, I boarded a train, not knowing where it was going. As the boat tilted to one side, where the shadowy fins were lurking, I remembered that train journey. Now I was on my way to another unknown destination, but would I get there?

Twelve hours had passed, and Al's eyes were focussed on the dirty sky straight ahead of us as if he were about to spot the ship at any moment. He appeared to have no interest in sustenance. The sun had been scorching us on the dhow's open deck all day, so it was a relief when finally it lost its intensity and disappeared behind billowing grey and red clouds. But the long night was not far behind. Al remarked that the lights of the *Flex LD* should be more visible in the dark and that would be when we would find her, but Hervé was agitated and anxiously looking out to sea in all directions. This restlessness caught on as I noticed the Indian mate doing so too. But looking did not conjure up a ship.

The groundswell was rising higher as the dhow slammed from side to side, grinding on into the night. The owner had not moved from the box; the glazed stare on his face was impossible to read, a determination to reach our destination? *Does he even know where our destination is?*

The band of red clouds was turning purple, the shimmering rim of the horizon began to fade, and I wondered what was going through Commander Jebsen's mind when the empty circle in his periscope suddenly focussed on a Liberty ship zigzagging its way over this same sea. Was it merely another prize for Germany? Or was he thinking about the men on board who he was about to blow out of the water? And what was going through Captain Ellerwald's mind on the bridge of the SS *John Barry* when the first torpedo hit? Did he believe they had a chance? All dreams would have been shattered in that one moment. Men scuttling up steel staircases chased by fire. Others racing to lifeboats, looking to escape. They knew the drill, but now it was for real. And all the while, Jebsen was watching through his periscope before releasing the next deadly torpedo. The ship broke in half and rose up against the sky before being sucked under, leaving a frothing whirlpool in its wake. Then nothing. *Until now.*

For now, the SS *John Barry* was stirring back to life in the lenses of the probes, hanging by a thread. And the contents of her holds might even find their way back to land. The mystery of the silver bullion was about to be uncovered. But would any of us on the dhow be there to see it? Darkness shrouded us, and the sea turned sinister, and with it came a squall, a fight and a flood.

Chapter Eleven

We were pitching violently. Figures morphed into shadows, obliterating their faces. The shadows moved uncomfortably around the boat. There were no lights, only the stars by which to navigate. Still, the little motor stuttered on endlessly outwards. Into the nightmare hours of an ink-black sea.

I manoeuvred myself next to Al, who seemed to have gone into another trance.

"How do these guys know where they are going?"

"I'm not sure that they do," he replied flatly, as though it were not for him to reason why. "They're fishermen; they are used to navigating by the coastline; this is way beyond what they are used to."

I froze fleetingly. "Doesn't that bother you a little?"

But he didn't answer, and if he shrugged, I couldn't see in the gloom. Hervé staggered over to tell me that darkness is depressing; it makes it seem that the weather is worsening.

"The weather is worsening," said Al.

All three of us believed we could see the *Flex LD* at various moments, but the stars, so plentiful and bright, were causing us to hallucinate. Stars were falling. Every few minutes, one would shoot across the matte black sky. Whole clusters of galaxies were looking down upon us. Laughing at us.

At around 8 pm, the squall was strengthening, and phosphorous foam flew past the gunwales. The boat's hull was crunching on the waves as if they were made of concrete, and the wooden bow splintered and gasped with the impact. The owner suddenly became very animated, calling for a tarpaulin to be pulled down from the mast. The mate swung around with a knife in his hand, narrowly missing Mac's head, but Mac was oblivious. The waves crashed over the bow, drenching the unconscious Richard, and Al remarked that if we couldn't find the *Flex* by midnight, perhaps we should turn north and head back. Hervé was infuriated by this idea. Goldie, who had got up to pray, asked if there was fuel on the drill ship as he didn't think we had enough on board the dhow to get back to land. This only enraged Hervé even more. Al calmly suggested that we should go in a ninety-degree box search pattern; that way we were bound to hit upon the *Flex LD*, to which Goldie lost the use of the English language and displayed no comprehension of what was being asked. Disgusted, Hervé retreated to the back of the boat to lie down.

We were lost. But no one would use that word.

I tried to settle down next to Mac; my mouth was dry, but I was outwardly calm. It was difficult to speak above the confused stream of gushing saltwater and the clanging of chains and ropes, all of which had taken over our boat and drowned out our plucky engine, which now appeared defeated in the mayhem. I put my arm around him, but any touch was of no comfort; we were alone. I secretly hoped we were now turning back, even though we would probably run out of fuel. This endless heading into an empty ocean with no land between us and the coast of Africa and very little chance of finding a ship was no longer the adventure I had anticipated. Fifteen hours had passed, so I had no doubt that we must now be well and truly beyond the *Flex LD*. *Madness.*

The arrangements had seemed vague. Even if those on the *Flex LD* had been expecting us, Rob might simply think that we had set off late. There were no lights on the dhow, so they could not possibly see us, and there would be another ten hours of darkness.

I saw my death certificate. *Death by drowning.*

I started to talk to myself, words of encouragement to block those negative thoughts as I plotted how to stay alive. A boat might survive a storm, but not the people on it if they were washed overboard. I decided to move to a plinth above the engine, where I lay in a puddle of oil and water. This was not the best idea, as the skipper constantly needed to go down a hatch carrying a hammer and a torch to check the engine, an excursion that was always followed by copious banging below. I looked around for the highest point. This was the highest point.

The picture of a child lashed to a mast came into my head. *The boy stood on the burning deck. The boy stood on the burning deck.*

Stop. Stop. Think how to save yourself.
The boy stood...the mast. My back against the mast.

If I can tie myself to… If I can reach for the coiled rope before it rears up. If I can wrap it around my waist and then to the mast. Uncoiling the rope, I tied it around my waist and then around the mast. A wave flung itself over the bow. *Lash the rope around the mast and hold on. Burning.*

Very hot air was coming from the hatch; the engine was overheating, and the fumes were overpowering. I looked around for the skipper, but he had disappeared.

Opening my eyes only seemed to make the weather worse. I tried to keep them closed. French swearing reached me through the sea spray. "*Putain, Merde, on va mourir!*" Then more raised voices. Arabic this time. I turned towards the source of the shouting. The owner and the skipper were crammed together in the wheelhouse. Two men at the helm, one tugging the wheel to port, the other fighting him to wrestle it in the opposite direction. Then, louder still, something exploded.

The engine stopped, and water spilled over the deck. The owner went into a state of panic, screaming and throwing his arms about, his eyes rolling in his head. This was it. We were sinking, and we had no life raft, not even a life jacket.

The skipper rushed to the engine, which he again proceeded to hit with his miserable hammer. The owner knelt down and cupped some water from the deck to his mouth and shouted to the skipper, who poked his head out of the hatch. Looking straight at me, he called out. "No problem! No problem. No sea. Water tank!"

Alarmed, I looked around for an explanation from Al.

He answered in his monotone voice. "I think it was the fresh water barrel that exploded; as long as they get the engine started again, we should be fine."

Good news.

Any hope of fresh water to last us several days had just departed, courtesy of a split barrel, and what was left was being bailed over the side and whipped back into my face by the wind.

Not such good news.

The storm was assaulting us head-on now. The deck was so low in the water that the waves were mostly above us. The sharks wouldn't have to wait long.

How easy would it be for a wave to reach over and draw one of us overboard? There was no chance of climbing back on board at night and not much chance in daylight either if the sharks had their way.

Black clouds were scudding past the moon, and the splintering of timber was louder still. The boat shuddered and twisted as we vibrated in the air. Rolling, squealing, shuddering. Then slosh. A wave was clawing at my clothes and shoes, trying to drag me away, but the rope held firm. I was drenched with a longing – a longing for morning, for dawn to release us. A canopy of stars was lowering itself; one by one, they separated until they were hanging beside me like a beaded curtain.

I closed my eyes and opened them again, and now I was between the stars, lost in the beads. I reached out to touch one and felt the warm night wind on the palm of my hand before drowning in salt.

The boy stood on the burning deck. The girl sits tied to the sodden deck. The wind drowns out voices. The wind drowns. I am on my own. Me and my rope. The rope holds me to the mast. Better to go under attached to the mast than washed into the ocean without it. What? But attached I was, and that is how I remained. Longing for the dawn. Darkness had fallen at 6 pm. Surely, it could not be long before daybreak. My watch caught the light of the passing moon. I tried to read it. The owner, who had been squatting nearby, leapt to his feet, put five fingers in my face and shouted five. His tone was so angry that I wondered if it was an offence to look at a watch. Could it be 5 am already? There was no dawn glow in the sky. Five hours to go? How would he know? I sneaked another look at my watch. A quarter to eleven. *A quarter to eleven!* Was that possible? Another eight hours of darkness to go?

Danger was rubbing its dirty paw against my skin; I had no control over where it touched me. We were spiralling through the waves on our way to nowhere, the tiny prop gasping for air as we leapt into a vacuum only to plunge anxiously into the abyss with a crash that shook every rusty nail in the dhow's timbered keel. A lifeboat-less splinter of rotting wood carried us above the stars. Each time we roller-coasted down, I expected us never to rise again. I shouted for flares, but no answer came, and I already knew the answer. I could just make out the skipper wrestling with the wheel. As for Mac and the others, I assumed they had either been washed overboard or were, like me, clinging to something that I hoped was not going to come away from itself. I gripped tighter on the rope and looked down the deck. I could just make out pools of water sluicing around Richard's lifeless body. At least he was still there.

A new fear gasped for air. What if no one was ever to find out what had happened to us? I was angry with myself about all the things I had not done. I had not left word as to the time we had departed or our destination. Why had I not made sure that the *Flex LD* was contacted to let them know we were due? Were they expecting us? Perhaps they were oblivious to us having ever left Mirbat.

My family would come searching, asking questions, trying to piece together the events that led up to this huge miscalculation, but nobody would be able to tell them what had really happened. Like so many before me, I would be one of those disappeared whose loved ones go looking but return with no answers. Anguished for the rest of their lives because there was no conclusion, no final moment of comprehension. Only doubt and heartache trailing behind them. Maybe a little less often as the years went by, but still lashing out from time to time all the same. And all because I didn't want to be perceived as weak, this worldly filmmaker, or was it for fear of being left behind and missing the adventure? Or worse, was it that as a woman I couldn't admit to being scared? I couldn't let my side down and say hang on a minute, is this boat seaworthy? Is it capable of a 200-mile voyage out into the ocean? My silence surprised me more than anyone, and now I was thinking, *Why did I agree to get into this fucking dhow?* We might have passed the *Flex LD,* and no one else was out here. Where was the radio contact? Where was a compass that didn't bounce around? *You idiot.*

To survive, you have to call out and not be afraid of being unpopular. You have to be the rogue monkey. The moment when I should have spoken up, I said nothing.

I yelled at the wind. *You idiot, you utter fool.*

When my moment came, I missed it. I stepped on board wordless, knowing all was wrong. Of course, this fishing dhow was not meant to take us to the *Flex LD*; it had been substituted for a launch that someone had decided was too expensive. Someone had palmed the hand of the local fisherman, pointed out to sea and said to take them there. I could see Gareth waving from dry land as we putted off to a watery grave. I was flooded with rage. Why did I place myself in danger just for the thrill of adventure? *To end like this.* No, it was not the drowning, but the ones I loved not knowing where I was, having to look for a corpse long eaten by the deep.

That, I really minded.

Chapter Twelve

When I was sixteen, I left school and travelled all over North America by Greyhound bus. In my classroom, nobody had yet travelled abroad, but all I could ever think about was the world beyond school. I would go as far away as possible and work wherever I could to pay for my journey, so when I saw an advertisement to paint the outside of someone's house in exchange for board and lodgings in Salt Lake City, I jumped at the chance and was soon there rubbing down the window sills.

The couple who owned the house were young. At the age of 28, Ralph Shuey was already a professor of archaeology at the State University of Utah, and his wife was a small, well-dressed Parisienne with a lapdog. After a few days with the sandpaper and the windows, Ralph announced that they were going to drive to the Four Corners, where the states of Utah, New Mexico, Colorado and Arizona all meet. There they would hook up with Doctor William Lipe and his students from New York State University on their search for artefacts from the Pueblo Indian tribe. Did I want to go with them? What other answer could there have been?

I sat in the back of the jeep with the dog, admiring the rock strata as it was pointed out to me. At night, we slept in the open on a tarpaulin under the stars. *Stars.*

Sixty miles from a little outpost called Mexican Hat in Utah, Bill Lipe had set up an archaeological dig and camp on a plateau beside a deep, dry canyon. Apart from sieving daily for the remains of a once-thriving Pueblo Indian community, his students were also exploring cave dwellings carved out of the canyon walls a thousand years earlier. It was agreed that in exchange for some sieving, I could have a tent and food, which meant that my house painting days, all five of them, were over.

The monotonous work in the sun was harder labour than I had anticipated, and the food every day consisted of tinned tuna and dry crackers, accompanied by rationed warm water from a leather bottle. But as I had no qualifications and no right to be there, I did not complain.

Bill's wife, June, was very welcoming and always upbeat. She tended to stay at the camp with her two children, where the artefacts, which consisted mainly of arrowheads we had found that day, were sorted and catalogued.

A bucket with holes in it was rigged at the bottom of the canyon and served as a makeshift shower, South Pacific style, except that the water gushed through so quickly there was no time for a song. Every morning, we banged our shoes in case a scorpion had snuck in during the night, and in the evening, we gathered around a campfire.

It was in Utah that I learned that humanity is divided between the creative whittlers who make up songs and the destroyers who like to torture scorpions by stinging them with their own tails. But no matter which side you are on, all prefer to taunt and tease one scapegoat rather than be that person themselves. Just as Golding described in *Lord of the Flies*, in a small, lawless community, one person is singled out as the victim. I observed and was relieved that I was not that person. I pitied the poor chosen student who did not fit in and kept my head down.

Perhaps Doctor Lipe sensed his students were spending too much time in close proximity to scorpions, or perhaps the tuna crackers and many consecutive days of tedium in the desert were the deciding factor; all we knew was that he gave us some time off so that we could explore the area more widely. Having spent many of my absent school days reading *The Rainbow* and *Women in Love*, I persuaded three of the students to drive me to Taos, New Mexico.

DH Lawrence wrote in one of his essays about New Mexico, where he visited in 1922, "I want to gather together about twenty souls and sail away from this world of war and squalor and found a little colony…a place where one can live simply, apart from this civilisation…"

Lawrence and his wife, Frieda, made for the *bohemian* town of Taos, where Mabel 'Dodge' Luhan, a prominent socialite, lived. On his return to London, he held a dinner party at the Café Royal, where he tried to recruit friends to move to Taos in order to create his utopian community. While almost all who attended agreed to follow him, when it came to the actual packing for departure, there was only one recruit – the Honourable Dorothy Brett.

In March 1924, Lawrence, Frieda and Brett arrived in Taos and stayed with Mabel Luhan. Initially, they all got along well, but tensions gradually built, and

Mabel, probably to stop Lawrence from leaving, offered him 160 acres located some twenty miles from Taos. Lawrence refused Luhan's offer, but it was accepted by Frieda, and they acquired the ranch in exchange for the manuscript of *Sons and Lovers*. After some renovations, the trio settled, with Brett taking the smaller of the two cabins on the property. She spent much of her time there painting and assisting Lawrence by typing his manuscripts and maintaining the property. She was also a skilful carpenter.

Early in 1926, Brett and the Lawrences travelled to the island of Capri in Italy, and from there, Lawrence and Brett travelled to Ravello, where they stayed together for ten days while Frieda remained on Capri. After Lawrence died, Frieda returned to Italy to be with an Italian lover who she later married, but Dorothy Brett went back to the ranch in Taos, where she lived alone, and that is where we found her.

Colourful in her Indian clothes and by now old and deaf, Dorothy Brett took extreme delight in showing three of us around. The fourth member of our group, Michael, decided to stay in the car, as he had never heard of D.H. Lawrence.

Surrounded by her artwork and clearly still in love with Lawrence, Dorothy was keen to talk about him at every opportunity.

"He had a vision, you see," she mused, her grey, rheumy eyes going into a dream of some past time that long ago had turned into desert dust. "He wanted to leave behind the smallness of the English mentality, so he came here to these wide-open spaces. But I was the only one who didn't leave," she added sadly before turning our attention to a stretched canvas on the wall.

Being a pioneer is lonely.

Over the years, she had immersed herself in her environment. The peaceful cave dwellers, who had lived at one time in that corner of New Mexico, had wandered into her paintings to be part of her life forever. We were so intrigued by this other world lost in time that we must have been with her for several hours, much to Michael's annoyance. As we got back into the car, he couldn't help but remark that had we left him hanging from a rope, he would be long dead by now.

Back at camp, Bill Lipe had somehow organised for us to visit one of the three sacred mesas on the Hopi Reservation in Arizona. Here, the Hopi tribe performs a religious ceremony every year that lasts sixteen days and concludes with the Hopi Snake Dance on the final day. The Hopis believe that snakes are like their brothers, and so they rely on them to carry messages down to the underworld, where the rain gods live.

Following in Lawrence's trail, our little convoy of jeeps found their way to the top of the mesa just as Lawrence's open-topped car had done many years before. The Hopis are strict about who visits them and, to this day, forbid any kind of photography. The only way to experience their secret ritual is to be present at it, and we were among the privileged few allowed to watch. We were advised to stay resolutely still, even when our instinct might be to run. We sat in a circle, rigidly cross-legged, on the sand. When it began, I realised it was exactly as it had been described in one of Lawrence's short stories. Nothing had changed.

"The boy launched his rattlesnake on the ground like a ship, and like a ship away it steered. Snake after snake had been carried round in circles, dangling by the neck from the mouths of one young priest or another…And before we realized it, the snakes were all writhing and squirming on the ground, in the white dust of meal, a couple of yards from our feet."

And that is what happened at the end of the dance we witnessed. All the snakes, fifty or sixty whip-snakes, bull-snakes and rattlesnakes, were thrown to the ground a few feet from where we were sitting and were sidling rapidly towards us. *Stay still. Don't move.*

At the last moment, as they were upon us, they were swiftly snatched up, curling and writhing in the arms of the priests, and were gone. Driving back to camp that evening, the imagery of the snake that had almost got to me had stunned me into silence. *Like a ship, away it steered.*

Hold on to the snake. No, hold on to the rope.

Two days later, there was a crisis in the camp. Everyone was going about their business after a day of sifting for artefacts in the field when, without warning, the sky turned an emerald green…and then black. Having never seen a sky that colour before, I was still staring at it when, in no time, it was over our heads. June, quick to react, called me into her tent with her two small children.

Emerald green sky. Emerald green waves.

Once inside, the storm struck. The ground beneath us shook as if in an earthquake. The tent collapsed on top of us, but we held it aloft with our hands so we could see the children and reassure them. But our hands were pummelled and pounded as though being pecked by a flock of crows. We refused to let go, and all the while, we both tried to laugh off the severity of the storm in front of the children until we were separated by the canvas disintegrating around us. I was on one side and the three of them on the other, but I could still hear June's voice calling cheerfully to them, "Well, isn't this fun?" The children saved us from fear. By reassuring them, we reassured ourselves. It is always better to protect than be protected. Our hands were stinging with pain, but we clung on until the storm, as abruptly as it had arrived, passed over us and was gone. The beaks ceased pecking and flew on.

The tent surrendered and limply draped itself over our heads.

"Are you still there?" said June.

"Yes," I replied.

The four of us crawled out from beneath what had once been the Lipes' campsite home and were confronted by a landscape we did not recognise. The desert was covered in large balls of ice. *An ice storm.*

The thunderclaps were diminishing, but now a different sound took their place: an unfamiliar roar. *The roar of water.*

Water in a desert? Where was everybody? We could scarcely make out voices over the boom of a gushing waterfall. Bill was rushing towards his family. Assured that they were safe, he turned his attention to his students.

"Anyone in the gully?" he called.

We ran towards our canyon, crunching frozen white foam beneath our feet. The ravine, which had been two storeys high, had disappeared and was now filled to the brim with violent, fizzing water streaking between our feet. Bill began to count. A boy was heard shouting that his girlfriend had gone to wash her hair in the canyon. He became hysterical. A search party was formed, and we spread out. *In a box.*

Alone in a white desert of crushed ice, it was easy to pick out a red gopher snake burrowing beneath a rock, but there was no other sign of life in my square of the grid. From the other side of the torrent came the shout that she was found. She had climbed out of the empty canyon when the ice storm struck and lay face down on the shelter-less plateau, covering her head with her hands when the hailstones attacked. Her hands swelled to twice their size, and by the time she was discovered, the back of her body was pitted with cuts and bruises.

Several days later, we found the shower bucket and the beer container a mile further down the ravine. A student called Teven and I were on a mission to alleviate the boredom of sifting for arrowheads when we found the battered bucket. Teven had spied some tiny caves high in a canyon wall and wanted to investigate. We discussed Vietnam as we climbed; he had no intention of ever being drafted. He would never go there. On our hands and knees, we crawled along a precarious trail, trying not to look down as we attempted to reach a dwelling carved into the cliff face. Inside the crude and miniature cave was a mummified baby wrapped in wicker, which she had lain in for hundreds of years.

And we had found her.

There was no room to turn around, so we shuffled backwards along the sloping track, and it was then that I fell and was suspended from the cliff face.

Chapter Thirteen

A wave hit me squarely in the face. The SS *John Barry* was out here somewhere. Had been on a night just like this. Captain Ellerwald. Twice, his ship had been torpedoed. What were the crew thinking when their ship was being ripped apart?

Will we be ripped apart? Will it ever be light again? The stuttering dhow threw itself at a wave and fought back. *Is hope gone?*

There is a line in *Persuasion*: *"All the privilege I claim for my own sex is that of loving longest, when existence or hope is gone."*

Over and over, this phrase repeated in my head.

At The Four Corners in New Mexico, the gravel along the trail to the cave dwelling had crumbled beneath me. I felt my feet sliding off the edge of the canyon. I clung to a sage brush root, sure I was about to drop to my death. In that one moment, I basked in the sunlight waving at me from the other side of the canyon, and I felt totally at peace with the world. A few seconds later, I was hauled up by Teven, who had very strong arms. He later lost one of them in Vietnam. As he set me down on the canyon's edge, hope returned, and I felt the pain and trauma of dying.

We spend our lives fearing death, but when it comes to the final moments, we give ourselves up to it. *We accept.*

Acceptance, the meaning of the word Islam. *Surrender to the will of God.* What is death? When it comes to it, it is nothing. A tip over the side, a suspended moment in the air. A sea of dead, sunken souls who have gone before in their millions. And yet we endure a lifetime of fear of being gone forever, taken by something that is over in a moment. *I should have listened.*

We can never avoid the inescapable end of the things we wish would remain. The concept of impermanence is central to Buddhism, in that the desire for an unchanging world is considered to be the greatest contributor to human unhappiness and pain. I was not about to reach nirvana. All my energy was concentrating on holding onto this rope. We cling to life because we don't want it to be over, and yet we know it will be; the curtain will come down at the end of the play, the coffee after the dessert.

I thought of my mother. Her ever-curious mind never seemed to grow old. We want to see how our children will turn out, but we are not content with that; we want to know how their children will turn out also. We want to be part of the future, not move over for it like everyone else in the history of the world has had to do. We want to be different. And most of all, we fear the manner of our going; we fear plummeting from that plane or being blown up in a shopping mall or sliding off the edge of a sea-sloshed dhow and not being able to breathe with lungs full of water.

How did this happen?

We don't even want to die in peace because we don't want to die, but we begin to think this is the best we can hope for, like dropping down dead doing something we love with a glass of champagne in our hand surrounded by our family, although the long goodbye is just as horrible. *Her hand turning cold in mine.*

And as our friends skittle over, who will be the last ones standing? Not the ones I expected and now, I thought, not I. Not like my grandmother, one of eleven children, attending her tenth funeral. Maybe sudden is better – harder for the ones who love us but better for us? My anger about no one knowing the circumstances of my death began to subside. A cloak of tranquillity wrapped itself around me as I made the transition into total acceptance of the inevitable.

I surrender. I accept.

And with acceptance, the waves backed away and left me alone.

The inevitable was broken by the sight of the skipper now standing over me, stargazing, or so I thought. For celestial navigation, dhow sailors have traditionally used a simple wooden device called a kamal that determines latitude by finding the angle of the pole star above the horizon. I hoped this was what he was doing and not just dreaming of home. I tried to speak to him, but he was too caught up with the stars, and he returned to his little box.

I focussed on my watch. I could almost read it. *Four? No, Five.* A muted red glow on the horizon was creeping ever so slowly towards the night sky, which was at last receding. *Daybreak.*

Daybreak was coming to rescue us. The walls of darkness that had enclosed us were retreating, and a grey-green ocean spread before us. A silver spray was visible. But there was no sign of any land.

The little engine had cut out, and the boat was rocking from side to side quite aimlessly, as if tamed by the approaching dawn. I released the rope so I could look around me and was relieved to see Richard on the foredeck, still there, still breathing in spite of the pools of water sliding around him. In the box, the head of the owner was buried beneath his mussar, resting on the wheel with the skipper asleep on his shoulder.

So far, four of us.

I reeled towards the side and crawled along between the nets to behind the wheelhouse. Mac, Hervé and Al were all asleep, stretched out between the debris, Al with his foot on the latrine. I tripped over Goldie, who was covered in a drenched tarpaulin.

That's eight.

"Mac. Mac."

Mac opened his sleep-filled eyes. He felt very sick. His wrist bands had provided no relief, nor had the patches.

"I thought I was gone," he whispered. "I tried to use the John, and a wave nearly pulled me under."

"Where's the bottled water from the hotel?"

"Over the side."

"What?"

"It got washed over."

"The Holiday Inn boxes?"

"Hervé threw them over."

I stared at him and then at the sleeping Hervé. *But why?*

"He was lying on top of them, and in a little Gallic fit, he threw them overboard."

"All of them?"

"All of them," was the reply.

One more to go. I went in search of the mate and found him fast asleep over the engine room.

I took stock. No missing men. No water, no food, no engine, no land.

At least, it was daylight. When you can see the rim of the horizon instead of menacing black waves a few feet away from your face, life regains some kind of normality where survival is possible. I made my way to the wheelhouse and poked the arm of the sleeping owner.

"Lost," he said almost robotically.

"Great," I said. "Any flares?"

Puzzled, he stared at me. I mimed firing a gun into the sky. He looked around and took a handgun from beneath some clutter.

"Oh well, if the worst comes to the worst, we can shoot each other."

He smiled blankly. At least he knew the word *lost*. I sat beside him contemplating the value of a gun when what was needed was radar, a transmitter or some form of communication, and failing that, some life jackets, a lifeboat with some oars, or a Holiday Inn sandwich and a plastic bottle of water, but a gun? Here we were, this little band of men and me, hanging aimlessly onto the swell from last night's storm, and the only bit of apparatus we had was a gun. It was then that I realised I needed the loo.

I staggered to the dipping kennel hanging over the stern and jumped in. As I squatted outside of the boat, the sharp pyramids of foam biting at my backside, I began to laugh at the absurdity of the situation. I clambered back on board; we were yawing from side to side, and I tried to keep my balance. The air was rapidly becoming roasting again, so I went to see Richard. His position had not moved, but I had no water to give him. Goldie stirred and went over to the burst water barrel, only to find it was empty. He looked wistfully out to sea. Used to navigating by the coastline, he too seemed disorientated. He prayed for a few moments then laid down again and promptly went back to sleep.

We drifted through the morning, hungry and thirsty and miserably lost. I surveyed the plane-less sky. *Nothing*. There was not a single shadow of a ship on the horizon either, not that we would be able to attract their attention without flares. *Nothing*. We were far away from the main shipping lanes, so the chances of seeing another vessel were always going to be remote. Even more remote were the chances that they would see us; we were no bigger than a cork long abandoned by its bottle. And even if they did spy us, it was well known that a tanker would often ignore a distress signal because of their tight schedule. If only we could communicate with the outside world, but then I could not communicate with the men on board, let alone the world. I considered the vastness of the ocean less sinister now but immeasurable all the same.

The skipper woke me from my trance. He held Mac's binoculars to his eyes. His deportment seemed different; his body was erect and alert. It was an age before he turned to me and smiled. He passed me the binoculars and gesticulated towards the pink haze. I held them up and adjusted them. *More haze.*

I turned the little wheel between the lenses. Creeping into focus was the sketchy outline of some mountains. Gradually, my body responded with a tremble, followed by nausea and a kicking in my head. I could no longer hold the binoculars. When hope returns, the solar plexus goes into shock. *The shock of being alive.*

Chapter Fourteen

There was much banging and hammering on the engine. Everyone was up now, animated and noisy, apart from Richard. The engine spluttered into life. Our Omani leader stood proudly on top of the wheelhouse as if nothing had happened to us and we were on some sort of pleasure cruise. It took an age for the mountains to make their presence real, but once we saw their leaden silhouette against the sky, we knew we would be safe. I sat on the bow for several hours, willing the coast closer. My once white trainers, now brown with tar and salt, stuck out in front of me like the sights on a rifle aiming at the land.

Another commotion led to the binoculars being frantically passed between the crew, and more arguing broke out over the terrain they were looking at. There were no lights to indicate our position, only a mist of mountains. Goldie said we were eight hours west of Raysut; someone else said we were too far east. The boat leaned one way then the other until the owner excitedly recognised something that alarmed him.

"Yemen," he said, pointing towards the landmass.

We turned sharply so that the mountains were on our port side. The Republic of Yemen was ravaged by civil war; the last thing we needed was to be caught up in someone else's conflict. The skipper's body language quickly changed. Having been completely out of his depth and unable to comprehend where we were heading, at last he was navigating along the familiar coastline.

He relaxed with the confidence and swagger of a man who knew his territory. There was also a sudden change of behaviour from Hervé too. I was gazing at the wake of the spinning spume glowing in the sunlight behind us now that we were moving again with purpose when he sat furtively beside me. He wanted me to know that there was nothing to be afraid of; it was only a storm.

Oh, is that what it was?

He told me it was better to be lost at sea than in the desert because at sea you are more likely to be picked up. *We weren't.*

Unfortunately, everything Hervé had said so far had proved to be wrong. Perhaps he needed to feel like he was in control, as it is always more comforting to protect than to be protected. I knew this from the children in the archaeological tent, whom I had once protected from the hailstones. Where were June Lipe's children when I needed them to make me feel brave?

By mid-afternoon, we were rumbling towards the military port of Raysut, Oman. No boat came to meet us. The little harbour was so sleepy that nobody seemed to notice us chug in. It was as though we had merely been out for an afternoon fishing jaunt. *Where is the search party looking for us?*

Silently, we moored. As we clambered onto the wharf, Mac fell to his knees and kissed the ground. The heat was crushing us, the land not steady enough to hold me. My legs shook, and my head spun. Richard woke up looking bewildered and then leapt up as though we had just arrived at our destination. Hervé disappeared to look for a phone while I sat on the quayside, trying to tame the ground beneath me. When I looked up, I saw a hearty Gareth approaching.

"I heard you were missing, but you are not missing at all! I was about to send out a boat to rescue you."

"Bit late for that," I replied.

Could it even be true? It seemed unlikely, but I was too occupied concentrating on my middle ear to question him.

"Seasick, Kate?"

"No. I don't get seasick."

"Were the lawyers?"

"Yes."

"Good," he retorted. "I hate lawyers."

Goldie lumbered over to us. "Time? Time we go back. Look for ship?"

Nobody answered him.

The air was over 100 degrees, and there was no shade. My head was pounding. The need for water took precedence over everything else. I was in the back of a car; we arrived at a hotel; it was not the Holiday Inn, so there must have been another one after all. *One that Gareth stays in?*

The Hamdan Palace Hotel was unfinished, but we were given rooms. Gareth commanded that we meet for dinner. "Debrief at 19.00 hours."

What? What was he talking about?

Silently, I staggered to my room. On the way, I met Mac. He was upset.
"All my clothes are soaking wet. How can I go to dinner in wet clothes?"

What?

"We have time, ask someone to dry them," I said helpfully.
"But they will need pressing as well."
"Well, I wish you luck with that." He smiled limply, and I watched him totter down the corridor, bewildered by his surroundings.

Inside my room, I went straight to the fridge, where I found two bottles of Evian. I devoured both of them and then looked ruefully at the empty plastic bottles. My holdall was too sodden to open. I wanted only to lie on the bed to stop my head spinning, but I was covered in oil and grease. My clothes were thick with the smell of the dhow. There was no hot water, but my body was too numb to care. Maybe it had gone into shock to protect me.

I could not feel anything. In a tepid bath, I tried to clean off the grey pit marks that had appeared all over me, as if I had been hit by hailstones, but now I saw that they were bruises.

If only the ceiling would just stay still for a minute.

The phone rang. It was Henry calling from Muscat.
"Welcome to Arabia," he chirped.

Nauseating.

"You know that you have cost the operation thousands and thousands of pounds." *Me?*

He wittered on, telling me that we had caused an international incident. I put the phone down. I left my room, very hungry, wearing a white hotel towelling dressing gown. I met Mac again in the corridor, who was also wearing a white gown. We stopped and looked at one another. Where were we?

Are we dead? Are we in a hell owned by Gareth and Henry? Or are we angels? We started to giggle, laughing at the absurdity of our situation. Two bruised bodies in towelling white dressing gowns who, a few hours previously, were thought to be at the bottom of the sea. We spontaneously embraced.

As two angels, we went down to dinner. There were no other guests in the hotel, apart from our disparate band of survivors. Richard and Commander Moore stood awkwardly in a deserted bar. Hervé was nowhere to be seen.

And Gareth was there; of course he was. "Ah, here you are," he barked. "Ready to go out again in the morning?"

Richard, who was still tinged with green from his *mal de mere*, replied enthusiastically that he was.

From the land finally beneath my feet, an electric surge rose through me before exploding into life. "What for Christ's sake were we doing on a fishing dhow that had no navigation equipment, no supplies, no life jackets, no flares and a crew with no clue as to where they were heading?"

"And a faulty rudder," Al added.

"What?"

"The rudder was useless; the chain was corroded and slack. I inspected it when I got off. It's a wonder the captain had any steering capacity."

"Captain?" I was cross, and not only with Gareth and Henry, I turned on Al. "Pity you didn't inspect it then before you got on. Isn't that your job, to check the seaworthiness of ships?"

"Only in the United States," he replied coolly. "I'm on a different mission here."

"Not much point to your mission if you never get there in the first place."

"Well, you're here now," Gareth said cheerfully, dismissing the outburst from someone I was sure he would later describe as a hysterical woman. At this point, Mac, who was still very upset about his ruined clothes, backed me up.

"We are not prepared to go out again on that dhow."

"No, we are not; we are not going on anything that isn't fully equipped with radar and lifejackets or isn't seaworthy," I said, furious now.

"Quite so," Gareth replied to the room in general. "Heads will roll. Now. Gentlemen, shall we eat?"

In the empty dining room, we were brought crayfish and beef, and plenty of beer was drunk. I was still trying to figure out why Gareth had turned up at the dock just as we were limping in. Or had he been waiting for some time? It was hard to tell; he was his cheery, blustery self, talking about silver bullion and how rich we would all be. Not strictly true if you were merely a camera crew, but the money was what mattered to the men.

Our ordeal was not referred to. But during dinner, a message was delivered to Gareth.

"So, gentlemen, it is all arranged," he announced. "An Omani Police launch, fully equipped with radar and lifejackets, and seaworthy, will be waiting for you in the morning."

He had heard me then.

"The car will pick you up at 4 am."

I could not imagine going out to sea ever again, but equally, I could not imagine not going either. The idea of never reaching the *Flex LD* after all we had been through was unthinkable. I had one last attempt to make him listen to me. "If we haven't arrived at the *Flex* by 3 pm, come and find us!"

But Gareth was his usual jovial British self.

"Oh, that was only a rehearsal for the real thing," he said, producing a map of the Indian Ocean from his inside pocket. He tapped it meaningfully with a glint of greed in his eye. "X marks the spot."

For a moment, I could have sworn I was looking at Blackbeard himself. And without a goodbye, he marched out of the hotel.

Chapter Fifteen

The police launch was an ex-British military boat with a fourteen-inch gun positioned on the bow, mainly used to deter gun runners selling weapons to Yemen. It was not big in size and quite low in the water, but it had a twin-screw engine and felt fast at fifteen knots as we soared out of the port and dipped in and out of the swell. The launch was fully equipped with a crew of eleven smiling, smartly uniformed Omani sailors. We were even brought a menu from which to choose our lunch, and tea was served in china cups. But this was by now our fourth day at sea, and the days still seemed long. Nobody said very much.

    I was offered a bunk and taken down to the V-shaped prow of the ship, where there were six bunks, all occupied. One of the sailors immediately jumped up and threw the Indian cook out of his bunk; it was then that I saw Richard was occupying one of the other beds. I declined their offer; besides, the bow was lifting and crashing down hard with a force so loud I preferred to be near the bridge.

    Hervé came to sit next to me, and after a long silence, he said, "Catrin, I feel a leetle bit guilty. I'm sorry."

    "That's all right, Hervé." I was trying to bury the image of our last water bottles from the picnic boxes floating on the Arabian Sea; perhaps we would pass them in our fancy launch. "But I will never go to sea in a fishing dhow again."

    He shook his head. "Nor me," he said.

    "But tell me, who is responsible for hiring the dhow and not supplying a military boat as we had been led to believe?"

    Now Hervé's expression changed to one that was very grave. He remained silent.

    So I persisted.

    "After all, isn't the Omani government supporting this enterprise? Money must have exchanged hands somewhere along the line."

Hervé shrugged in a typical French way. I could see he was not going to give me an answer, and I was too tired to continue.

After nine slow hours, Mac nudged me and pointed to the radar screen. I could just about see a tiny dot in the centre of a circle, but when we looked outside, we could see nothing. Even though the *Flex LD* had a tall derrick, inside of which was the drill pipe, you had to be well within range to see it from such a low vantage point. The visible distance is fifty miles on a clear day, but the lower you are in the water, the less you can see. Had we been even within a few miles' radius, we were destined never to find it from a tiny boat without radar. The true reality of our senseless mission was beginning to sink in. I stared thoughtfully at the screen as we headed towards the dot, but peer as I might, there was no sign with the naked eye, or even through binoculars, of the *Flex LD*.

Two hours of staring later, we were within a radius of nine miles, and I could just make out the ship's derrick swaying like a pendulum on the horizon.

"There," I called, "over there, the *Flex*." Richard, too lazy to leave his bunk, shouted up to me.

"What does it look like?"

"Like the Eiffel Tower!" I shouted to him. "We are nearly in Paris."

Another hour and we were closing in on a ship dominated by its tower that now loomed above us. The *Flex LD* had been stationery since it had arrived at its satellite position. Not that it could ever be still, currents and waves will endlessly throw any ship off course. But the *Flex LD* was equipped with four main thrusters that were continually cutting in against the elements every time the ship veered from its position. The result was a ship that was uncomfortable in its own element. Unable to sail, it was tethered to a wreck over a mile and a half below on the ocean floor by a drill *string* consisting of pipes screwed together at 90-foot intervals. The pipes took 10 hours to dismantle before *Flex LD* could ever set off again. *Let alone search for a missing dhow.*

As we drew alongside the red, rusting portside hull, I felt very small. High above us was a rail of faces watching but not smiling or waving, simply gawping at us. Most of the faces were either Indonesian or Filipino and had been collected together in Singapore. All were male, and all were wearing white hard hats and orange overalls. *That's a lot of men.*

The strong smell of grease and oil was overpowering after the sweetness of the salt air. Amongst the faces, I noticed a white face wearing a red hard hat, also in overalls but wearing shorts and yellow sea-boots. He, too, was staring. It was not the welcome I had been expecting. Then I recognised Jay filming us and a solemn Brian Shoemaker looking on. *At least, I know two of them.*

A Jacob's ladder was lowered. Our boat was lurching in an attempt to stay alongside. An abyss opened up between the launch and the ladder, and there was nothing for it but to leap and be sure to snatch hold of a rung. Our belongings, including my camera case, were hauled up by rope and dangled precariously over the side before being hoisted onto the main deck.

The man in yellow sea boots was Rob Hudson, and he greeted me with a grim: "We thought we'd lost you."

"We thought so too," I replied, shaking his hand, relieved to be so high above the ocean. There was no other salutation from anyone else.

"Ignore them," Rob said. "They are a superstitious lot."

Of course, the old superstition about a woman on board a ship. *But really?*

"They have been razzing about it for days, but now that you are here, they don't know what to do. Come, I'll show you your quarters."

As we went to go below, I could see Jay and Brian hugging Mac. Rob led me down some grey metal corridors until we came to an oblong door with a high sill to step over. So this was the Rob Hudson I had heard so much about. He was shorter than I had imagined, with blonde, spikey hair and tanned skin. The man who was in charge of this whole operation was more like a barn owl than the eagle I had been expecting. His warm brown eyes looked at me with concern.

"I kept this one for you; I hope it is all right."

"Yes," I said gratefully before stepping inside. "I was expecting I might have to share."

"Really?" My comment surprised him. There was an awkward moment when neither of us knew what to say.

"Hard hats and boots on deck at all times," he said, and with that order, he left me there.

I looked around at my new home. A worn-out operating table with a black plastic cover, a few instruments on a shelf but no medical supplies. I had been given the hospital quarters. In the corner were two bunk beds, *all mine,* and in another, a toilet. The porthole was well above sea level, but it didn't open. The air was stifling. There was no air conditioning, not even a fan.

When I opened the door, a Filipino man wearing a grubby apron was outside, grinning. "Hello. I'm the cook; this is my cabin opposite." He leered at me in a way I didn't really warm to.

I glanced at my door. *No lock.*

"Good. What's for dinner?"

"Plenty."

"Good."

I went in search of someone I knew. Where was Mac, the only one I could call a friend? I found him on the boat deck.

"Well, this IS the adventure," he said. He seemed overjoyed that we had finally reached our destination. Brian and Jay had been showing him around, and he wanted me to see them before their departure. I expected to be greeted with disappointment from the two men who had no choice but to return to Oman on the police launch; instead, I was welcomed warmly.

Brian was delighted to see we were still alive. "I was very concerned when you didn't show up. I tried to contact the U.S. Navy, but they wouldn't let me. I'm sorry that we're reunited for so brief a time."

Jay was like a puppy jumping up and down at his owner's return, as excitable as ever. "They think they may have seen coin boxes in one of the holds."

Brian nodded sagely. "Could be. Could be."

We visited the small, dark monitor room where Jean Roux, the salvage master, was scrutinising a screen. He did not look up at us when we entered, but I could faintly make out his silver hair and chiselled chin in the half-light. All was silent, certainly no greeting. All eyes were on the black-and-white video screen, where the images were noticeably murky. To the naked eye, it was a challenge to see anything other than swirling mud and debris.

Outside, I had my first glimpse of the moonpool. A perfect circle positioned right below the derrick, with pale turquoise water lapping inside. *A ship with a hole in its middle.* It could almost be mistaken for a swimming pool on another kind of ship, but not here. This pool could reveal the deepest secrets of the ocean.

We brushed past some of the workers, their eyes warily following me as I lagged behind the four reunited Americans, who swiftly climbed up and down steel ladders and along the decks, for this was a whirlwind tour. The launch was waiting to depart with Brian and Jay. There was only time to take a photo of the four of them together. Brian unfurled the Explorer's Club flag, and all four beamed at the camera. *Snap.*

A driller was waiting for them on the main deck. He was carrying a rucksack and had a heavily bandaged hand. A few days before, it had been cut open on a piece of machinery that was hauling pipes. He was about to be sent ashore for treatment. There would be one less man on the rig. It was then that I realised why the hospital cabin was free. *There is no medic on board, no one to help us if we are injured or sick.*

Jay and Brian put on brave faces as they stood by the gangway, preparing to depart. Having missed out on the surveillance ship when they first visited Oman, how hard must it have been for them now to leave before a single coin had been retrieved? They had been gearing up for this moment for so many years, only to have to leave it all behind. But that was the deal with the Ocean Group, only two of the JB4 on the expedition at one time. And this whole enterprise was all about deals. Just as my deal was to make a feature that would launch my production company.

On his first trip to Oman, Jay had videoed their visit. He now handed me a VHS neatly labelled *The Oman Caper*.

"Here, you complete the film," he whispered to me.

I thought of my Hi-8 camera sweltering on the hospital bed in my cabin, having barely survived the salty dhow *caper*, let alone this one. I promised him I would do my best. Inside, I was swirling with self-doubt because the only record of this million-dollar treasure hunt was down to me.

One by one, as if being led to an execution, they descended the rope ladder and swung heavily onto the foredeck of the launch.

Having appeared from nowhere at my flat in London, they seemed even more incongruous now, a pair of veterans bobbing about on the Omani police boat that had, only some hours earlier, delivered us on to the iron deck of the salvage ship, from which I was now looking down on them. I was the latecomer, a stage hand, a pretend cameraperson, not a treasure hunter or an entrepreneur. But I was also the lone representative of my gender on board the *Flex LD*.

I waved and waved at the two men fluttering their Explorer's Club flag above their heads as the launch pitched its way into the distance. I could just about make out Jay's silver hair and the flag still held aloft as they dissolved into the setting sun. I turned to Mac as if to speak, but he was staring beyond me at the wide ocean that had swallowed them up. The two old timers had been replaced by us, and the hunt for the treasure would go on without them.

Chapter Sixteen

The *Flex LD* was a working ship that operated 24 hours a day. On board, there were seventy-five men and me, and that is the way it would stay for many weeks, maybe months, to come. Men slept while others worked, depending on their shifts, but every one of them had a role to play, and they viewed me suspiciously. I was the siren who had to be approached with caution.

One exception was the electrical engineer, who was strong and stocky with a scar across his nose. He had shaggy hair and a bushy moustache. His overall was bright blue, with the name *Wayne* penned in black ink above the pocket.

"G'day! I see we have another pom on board." I had walked around a bulkhead and straight into him on the boat deck.

"So you must be Australian?"

"Yeah, proud to be the only Aussie on board the *Flex*. I've come on deck for some peace."

"What?"

"I've come out here for some peace," he shouted above the noise of the screeching pipes.

"Really?"

"Yes, much quieter than in that baking-hot engine room. Never stops down there; can't hear yourself think."

"I find it hard to sleep in my cabin, and it's not even near the engine room. Must be hell down there," I shouted back. I didn't tell him the real reason my sleep was disturbed. Alone in my bunk, memories of the dhow shuddered and shook me awake.

"S'aright. I was in the Australian Navy in Vietnam, serving on a destroyer. The guns would go off all night, but I was so dingo tired I would fall asleep on the gun turret."

"That's incredible," I said, "even if you were exhausted."

"When the guns stopped firing, the silence would wake me. I guess I had become so accustomed to the noise. Now I sleep to the sound of a diesel engine beneath me, and the only time I find it hard to sleep is in the quiet of my own home."

He laughed to himself and went on his way. At least he was a friendly face, for I could sense the tension on board, not without reason.

The first tropical depression passing over the area for fifty years had marooned us on the dhow with its strong winds and high swells, but it had also slowed the salvage operation almost to a halt. This had not lightened the mood. By the time I arrived on board the *Flex LD*, the decks of the SS *John Barry* were still being cleared, and nothing had been retrieved. In a matter of a few weeks, the monsoon season would be upon us. The pressure was now on to salvage the coins and then look for the bullion before the storms came, when it would be impossible to hold the ship in place. The stakes were too high to contemplate failure. The silver had to be salvaged or money would be wasted, careers ruined, men broken. *Will they blame me if it was all for nothing?*

"We will find it," said Rob confidently. "We have to."

On my first day, I went up to the bridge. The captain, Captain Paul, greeted me. His English was almost non-existent, and his French was very gravelly, almost indecipherable, even to his small band of French officers. He stuttered and smiled his way through conversations that appeared to be ignored. It was clear that he had little to do but hover over his DPS crew, who were glued to the monitors and barely noticed him.

The ship had nowhere to go, which meant that Captain Paul's responsibility was to stop us from veering away from the small cross on their screen. Day and night, they had to be vigilant.

We were constantly in danger, for if the pipe that tethered us to the wreck was not cut loose in a violent storm, the ship could be dragged under.

I retreated to my quarters, where I picked up the stained and salty camera bag and held it to me. Inside, the Hi-8 camera was still intact, or so it seemed. I pulled out the cables, tapes, batteries and the microphone, which I gaffered onto the top of the camera. Without these, I had no right to be there. I unzipped my sodden holdall and released the awkward-fitting hard hat and the boots that had been hastily crammed into it at the last minute. I laid out my few pieces of clothing—some shorts, a t-shirt and some underwear—on my bunk and immediately wished I had packed more. With my mind on the absence of network funding and a camera crew, it hadn't occurred to me how long I might be away. I had already lost track of time; my life in London seemed a long time ago.

I looked around; there was no soap or shampoo, not even a towel. Amongst my few possessions was the damp, treasured copy of *Persuasion* with its turned-up corners and well-thumbed pages. I removed it carefully and opened it on a random page. *"I must go, uncertain of my fate."* I placed it by the bunk to dry out.

I made my way to the upper deck and found Mac's cabin. It was much larger than mine, but then he owned the wreck, or at least he did once. His crumpled clothes were now in neat piles on his bed. I was impressed that he had brought so many. The contents of his sponge bag were carefully laid out by the sink. He gave me one of his soaps and a sachet of shampoo, and I left him, wishing I had some clothes to change into.

Dinner that evening in the mess started badly. Animated conversations melted into furtive mumblings as I entered for the first time. I queued up behind some oily overalled men, and the cook winked at me as he sloshed an extra-large portion of curry, which I was never going to eat, into a bowl. I was aware of a posh British voice quite loud above the others. Major David Hopps, who was in charge of security, was the only cheery person in the mess and seemed to be unthreatened by my presence.

"Ah, another Brit on board to swell the ranks. Splendid. Come and join me for a beer."

There was no bar on board, as Henry had said there would be; only one can of beer or coke was permitted daily.

"It's amazing how long you can make a can of beer last," he said; it was a challenge to be relished as far as he was concerned.

"Would you like mine as well?" I said, as really, I would have preferred a bottle of water.

"Not allowed. Would have to walk the plank if I had two," he retorted, his face alight with mischief. I sat with him, sipping very slowly from my can.

"So…why are you sitting in a mess so far from anywhere, drinking rationed beer?"

"I could ask you the same question," he came straight back at me.

"That's a long story."

I thought for a moment about where I would begin. *Where does any story begin?*

"Well, mine is short. I'm a British ex-army officer from Suffolk. I diffused bombs in Northern Ireland, and I'm now for hire. And they hired me."

Part of the reason for the Major's cheeriness was that he was being paid to do nothing, and this suited him very well. He was on board to count and guard the coins.

"Do you believe there will be any to count?" I asked him.

He shrugged. "Makes no difference to me either way."

Although he was very friendly to me, he was also indifferent. It wasn't personal; he was indifferent to everyone, preferring not to engage beneath a superficial level. At least my presence didn't stop him from swearing, whereas the Americans and Dutch on board apologised every time they swore in my hearing, which soon became tedious for all of us. His sidekick, Tom, who sat silently at the same table, was less cheerful, a younger ex-serviceman, blonde and a bit miffed as to why he was cut off from the world with nothing to do. Together, they were referred to as the *Army Boys*.

At first, I thought I should be seen filming, but I had to remind myself that my tape stock was limited. *Why did I bring such a small supply?* I gravitated towards my hospital quarters to hide from the men, but that was not always possible. The air in the cabin was often above 100 degrees, so I climbed a steel ladder to a deck above the bridge, otherwise known as the monkey island, and dragged an old plastic chair into the shade of one of the bulkheads.

From there, I could watch the skinny but surprisingly strong Indonesian workers tirelessly attaching the pipes to each other on the drill deck. With a grunt and a sigh from the machinery, each pipe was lowered by three metres, then screwed to the next, letting out a piercing scream as it tightened. This relentless process would go on until the grab reached its ghostly destination beneath us. The clanging and screeching of pipes and the roar of the thrusters became the sounds of my world.

Once the drill pipe reached the wreck, work could begin lowering the grab into the hold a few metres at a time. This was when the atmosphere was the most on edge, as it required concentrated precision and was the reason the salvage master, Jean Roux, never looked up when I crept into the monitor room pretending to film. With it taking nine to ten hours to lift a load to the surface, he had to be sure he had something worth bringing up.

I watched as he carefully cleared a path to Hold Number Two, depositing the contents into a huge metal skip that had previously been placed on the seabed to bring up at a later date. I stood silently a few feet behind him and wondered why, having invested millions in the recovery vessel and the design of such powerful equipment, they had not invested in some better cameras to place inside the jaws of the grab.

For long periods of time, you could see nothing at all. Occasionally, a murky shape would swing into view, but the visibility was dire. Each time Jean Roux removed some deck cargo from the upper deck of the SS *John Barry*, swirling sediment would follow and take up to four hours to clear.

Mac and Richard were often in the control room watching too, peering over Jean Roux's shoulder, hopefully. I longed to see the grab up close, but it was some time before it was due to surface, and so many hours were spent on deck waiting.

Another steaming hot day forced me from my cabin, and I went along to the mess to make myself some breakfast. The cook was there with his helpers.

"What is your name?" he called.

"Catherine."

"Katee."

"Katee then, yes. What's yours?"

"Cookie." He laughed. "Call me Cookie."

I laughed too. Exhibiting some fake confidence was paying off, and although I couldn't be sure, the staring seemed to lessen with every next visit to the mess.

On my way to my plastic chair, I passed a meeting room that was all white. White tables and chairs and a large whiteboard on which someone had sketched diagrams of the original plans of the SS *John Barry* in red pen. When I looked in, I saw Rob was alone, studying the board. I tentatively asked him if he was aware, at the time of our first journey to the *Flex LD,* that we were lost.

"Yes, but we were expecting a naval vessel, not a fishing dhow."

"Yes, so was I." *Should have said something.*

"You were lucky. Two Indian fishing boats disappeared that night and never returned to port. They had sent a Mayday signal, but no one came to their rescue." Ruefully, he added, "Their government decided they weren't worth the fuel." *Who is?*

Just then, Captain Paul appeared, followed by Eric, an expert advisor on salvage operations and techniques from Holland. Eric always wore orange overalls, perhaps because he was Dutch. His hair was grey and so was his bushy moustache. He reminded me of an oversized Scottish terrier.

I stayed in the room. No one asked me to leave. The two Ifremer men, Pierre Valdy, the passionate grab designer, and Jean Roux, entered and sat down in silence. These two men could not have been more different and yet their commitment to their company was very apparent. They believed wholeheartedly in the project. The grab was made in France, and its success was never in doubt.

Next to enter the room was Brad, the operation's tool pusher; he nodded at me as he took his seat. Brad was a Texan with a deep southern drawl and, at first, very few words. He liked to wear cowboy boots when off duty so everybody would know where he was from. He was wary; I could feel his discomfort, and he was definitely very reluctant to be filmed. With the men, he exuded confidence because on an oilrig the tool pusher is of the highest rank after the captain and in charge of the drill crew. This would explain Brad's superior demeanour, as arguably he had the most important position of all; he had the potential to make both the Ocean Group and the JB4 very rich.

Rob was under immense time pressure; he alone had to make a decision as to whether to extend the operation, as so far nothing had yet been found. A heated French exchange ensued between Captain Paul and the two men from Ifremer, who took centre stage.

"Please, gentlemen, let's conduct this meeting in English; we are an international team, and blaming each other is not helpful," Rob interjected calmly but firmly.

Jean Roux scowled. "We have lost three whole days due to the satellite navigational equipment not being accurate enough to keep us exactly over the wreck," was his cold reply.

The Captain objected passionately, but his English was inadequate to express his side of the argument, and he floundered, trying to explain to the bemused assembly. In the end, he resorted once more to speaking French, which had to be translated for the benefit of the English, Dutch and Americans. He insisted that his men were doing sterling work, keeping us constantly in position and added in a last-ditch attempt at English: "And we also lost time waiting for the stupid dhow that never showed up." *Are we supposed to apologise for being alive?*

Rob intervened. "On a positive note, today we saw what looked like the remnants of boxes on the grab camera."

Pierre leapt on this. "Coin boxes?"

Jean Roux shrugged and aimed his comment at the Captain. "There was too much sediment to be sure because we were moving around too much. The debris had to be deposited into the skip."

Before another slanging match kicked off, Eric prodded his sword into the fray.

"Had the Dutch designed the grab, it would have been much better."

Pierre leapt to his feet and began to prance around the room, declaring that his grab was the first of its kind and had never been tried at such depths. I wondered if Eric had wanted to cause a row, just to relieve the boredom. Pierre went on. "It can tear open steel decks with its teeth and pick up the contents beneath and 'old them in its jaws. Zere is nothing wrong with zee design."

Except for the camera inside, which is blurry. Say nothing.

Jean Roux suddenly became aware of me sitting silently in the corner.

"Are you filming this?"

"No," I lied. One trick I had taught myself was to cover the red recording light with black gaffer tape so that they couldn't tell whether I was just holding the camera or filming for real. The focus was now on me, and the grab competition subsided. Rob told everyone to sit down.

Jean Roux continued to address the room. "When we were clearing a few hours ago, I may have seen box-shaped objects in the aft corner of the tween deck, but nothing is certain. It is up to you, Rob. Do we go on or retrieve?"

Rob had to weigh up whether to go for what Jean Roux may or may not have seen in the swirling mud or delve deeper. The research he had done, combined with Brian Shoemaker's, led him to believe that they were now closing in on the coins. For a few moments, he looked away, his thoughts far from the room, from the ship, even from the ocean.

Everybody waited in silence.

"Go on with the clearing," he said at last.

The men traipsed off to their cabins, taking their solitary thoughts with them, leaving me alone staring at the red ink on the white board. I could just make out the faded line where it had been wiped away, signifying the SS *John Barry's* main deck now smashed and peeled open by the grab.

Underneath was a tween deck and then Hold Number Two. Was Rob right? Was this where the strongroom should be? I thought of the men who had loaded the ship that distant night in Philadelphia. What would they make of this destruction? Would they cheer for the recovery of their lost cargo or prefer their secret to stay under the sea?

Chapter Seventeen

As darkness descended, I lay in my bunk, listening to the groans of a ship struggling to stay in one place. There was more movement than usual, and the sea was hurtling against the thick glass in my only porthole. At least I hoped it was thick. Large waves struck the hull and killed any chance of sleep. *Another squall, perhaps?* I pictured the dark under those low-hanging stars and the clouds racing above and shuddered. The blackness was descending underneath the thin skin of the ship. Then nothing but water until the murky ocean floor.

There was nobody on board with whom I could share my isolation, and once more I questioned how I had come to be here. I had abandoned my empty office, my tiny flat and my complicated love life, and now I was marooned on a static ship in the middle of the ocean. It may as well have been a desert island with no means of making a raft or passing ships to semaphore for help. Escaping a cyclone was no better than being in the eye of one. Eventually, the shaking subsided and morphed into the noise from the *Flex's* engine room, where Wayne would be fast asleep.

I must have drifted off, for without warning, I suddenly sat bolt upright and looked around my cabin in the blue neon light that never went off and remembered where I was. The emptiness of loss had crept into my dreams, only to be still there, staring at me from the vacant bunk above when I awoke. Loss is nobody expecting you to arrive.

I picked up my book and began to read and was transported back to land.

"She was persuaded to believe the engagement a wrong thing – indiscreet, improper hardly capable of success, and not deserving it."

A persistent banging on my door broke into my trance.

It was Mac, and he was excited about something unusual showing inside the grab.

I must come immediately and film.

I dressed hurriedly into my blue dungarees, boots and hard hat, snatched up the Hi-8 camera and ran to the control room. Mac, Richard and Rob were all gathered behind Jean Roux, staring at the murky screen. Roux knew exactly what they were looking for. Each wooden box weighed roughly one hundred and fifteen pounds and was stencilled with various contract and requisition numbers, a case number and the word *Dhahran*. Rob pointed to just inside the jaws, where we could make out the letters DHA burned into a piece of wood. We could hardly breathe in the solid air.

I picked up the camera to focus on the monitor and peered through the viewfinder.

Black.

I quickly changed the battery; the red light for recording was on. Still black. Then it went dead. *Nothing. Dead. Completely dead.*

I frantically fitted another battery, all the while trying not to draw attention to the dead piece of kit in my hands, trying not to show that I was now going hot and cold and starting to panic. Despair struck me with a hideous blow of realisation, pain and fear, greater than the shark-infested dhow-tossing ocean. That experience had been surreal.

This was real. Everyone doing their duty. Except me.

Why had I only brought one camera? Why had I not brought a spare? How was I going to explain this catastrophe to anyone? What other reason was there for me being there? There was only one thing for it: pretend to film.

The decision was made to bring up the grab. I had nine hours before I would be found out. I had never felt more lonely in my life. In whom could I confide? After a few sweaty hours of pacing in my cabin, I decided to approach Wayne. He was in charge of the rig's electronics after all.

Tentatively, I knocked on his cabin door. Wayne was doubtful at first without diagrams to follow, but either he felt sorry for me or he liked a challenge. He rested the camera carefully on his desk and painstakingly began to take it apart. Wayne had fat fingers that were at odds with such delicate work; they were more akin to huge hydraulic machinery, but he patiently dismantled the camera, which was worth more than me as far as Gareth was concerned. It was bad enough having a woman on board.

But a pointless one?

It was as if my body were being laid out on a shroud, ready to be dissected. Every tiny screw Wayne extracted, he placed in a precise order so that it could go back the same way.

"Never worked on a machine this small, not my speciality."

I smiled faintly. I even considered fainting so as to be oblivious to what was happening. He looked up over his half-glasses when I didn't answer.

"Every part has a logic, and as long as I can put it back together again, we have a chance."

A chance? I observed helplessly as the reason for my being there sadly disbanded into a hundred pieces. I felt more lost now than I had felt on the dhow; it was more than a camera. My insides were spilling across Wayne's desk, and I was at his mercy. *You are thousands of miles from anywhere, you have one mission, and you brought one camera.*

"Ah," Wayne said at last in his thick Aussie accent, "there's your problem right here."

I stared at my remains.

"The salt didn't help."

So I had survived the dhow, but my camera hadn't survived the salt and the damp. I should have covered this precious piece of kit during the squall instead of Richard, who was very much alive now and an even bigger pain in the arse than he was before.

"She's right. I'll have her back together in no time."

"Really?"

Hope can be a terrible thing.

"Sure, just need to dry her out a bit. The extremes in temperature can cause condensation."

He took hold of a cloth from his glasses case and began to wipe each element, then he bridged two modules with very fine fuse wire, so fine it was hardly visible. I watched with mounting tension as he carefully and methodically put all the elements back together. Finally, after several hours, the surgery was over. The camera sat whole again on his desk. He attached a battery, tapped the switch and it whirred into life. I began to breathe again. I was so grateful; I was in love.

Wayne was now my best friend. He showed me pictures of his daughter and told me how well she was doing. He talked about his divorce and how he had recently met a girl and couldn't wait to see her again. He was thankful that there was now somebody on board this ship who he could talk to. His gratitude was nothing compared to mine.

As I left with my working camera in my hand, we agreed never to utter a word about our time in his cabin together.

"...when pain is over, the remembrance of it often becomes a pleasure."

Beneath the drill deck and the continual cranking and screaming of drill pipes, I set up my tripod and spent the next few hours staring into the pale turquoise moonpool, waiting for something other than pipes to appear. One by one, men arrived to wait with me. Richard and Mac looked on anxiously.

The leviathan was making its way towards us. I did not know what to expect, but a tremor of foreboding shook the deck as the grab worked its way towards the open moon pool.

Finally, the shiny domed top of a missile-shaped pod came into view. Oozing and hissing, a bright yellow capsule emerged reluctantly through a thrashing sea. I had seen drawings but not the real thing, and I was surprised at how unscathed the pod appeared considering the depths from which it was returning. Inside were the cables and lighting that made it possible to view the interior of the grab when it was over a mile below us.

A dark, threatening shadow followed, a steel, black monster loitering under the ship. I was about to have my first sight of Pierre's proud invention. The fifty-tonne spitting beast kept on coming, straining to breathe after its long and perilous journey through the ocean. It groaned and screamed under its own weight as it was winched out to dangle precariously above the pool.

Machinery grinded and whistled into action. The platform beneath my feet rumbled and rocked as the giant was restrained with hooks and pulleys attached to cranes, which heaved and hauled until it was over a vast metal tray that had been placed on the deck. Here, it swung lifelessly from side to side. Trapped in its teeth was the carcass of part of a Liberty ship. The splintered remains of rotting wood oozed a sulphuric black stench, the trapped last gasps of a ship's crew once on duty.

Seawater gushed from the jaws until it subsided into long, slow drips. After a motionless calm, the jaws cranked open to release the planks of chewed wood, which crashed into the tray, followed by mangled steel and debris.

A worker picked up a soldier's helmet and tossed it to one side; it rolled and settled at my feet. I knelt down and held it close to me. *Whom had it belonged to?*

Men were shining torches inside the monster's mouth.

"Nothing there!" one shouted. *Nothing? Whose helmet was this?*

Then another excited shout. Suddenly, Rob and several men in red overalls were clambering through the stinking debris, their heads disappearing inside the jaws. I released my camera from the tripod and followed Rob into the tray.

"Anything?"

"No," said Rob. "But I'm convinced we are near."

"How do you know?"

"I can smell silver."

Chapter Eighteen

As the grab made its long descent back to the wreck, it was impossible to know when there would be anything to film again, so I searched for places to conceal myself. I clambered over anchor chains, capstans and stanchions onto the mass of rusty red and white metal that was now my home in the bow. The foredeck is the quietest part of the ship, and here, I felt the freest and the most private.

Ahead of me, there was no trace of human life, but I was high enough up not to feel threatened by the sea. I could imagine the bow wave dividing either side of the prow as it cut through the ocean and dolphins leaping through the spray on our way to some faraway land, but instead the bow was stationary. I looked back at an empty bridge and remembered that we were not going anywhere. Asking a ship to be stationery is like being asked to tread water. *Eventually, you will drown.*

When I grew tired of imagining this magical voyage we were on, I headed for the deserted helideck at the stern. It was always empty, except I once saw Al up there jogging around the perimeter. Exposed to the elements, I trod carefully as if I were standing on Beachy Head, peering over the edge to see what falling might be like. The flat, square tabletop was not protected; you could end up over the side if the wind caught you right. And then there was always the danger of the magnetic depths forcing me to look down, *forever down*, where my mind capsized and I was below the hull, sinking for more than a mile until I was inside the Liberty ship, buried in silt, buried in history.

Having explored all corners of the ship, I retreated to my lone chair on the monkey island to read. I had no sooner opened *Persuasion* than I felt the presence of a man breathing behind me as he stood immobile, wondering how to begin his approach. There was no other chair or couch for him to lie on. He stood awkwardly, shifting his weight from leg to leg like a boy needing the toilet, before stepping a little closer, pretending to be interested in the book I was reading.

Shiftily, he looked over at the pipe activity on the rig platform, in case he was going to be caught out by another crew member, before making his move. But action on the drill floor stopped for no one, and he was quite safe. Then he would begin. *To confide his secrets.*

Macho bantering mess-man started slowly with small talk before slipping into sentiment. He wanted to talk about his family. His wife, whom he missed but who didn't understand him; his children, who did not need him anymore now that they were grown up; and his mother, who used to make him apple pies that no one else could make.

Mother. Always Mum.

A journalist once told me that when he had been captured filming behind enemy lines, he had been in prison with the toughest of men who could endure their torturers, but in their sleep, they called out for their mothers. There was no torture here. No uniting against outside forces, just isolated thoughts longing to share with another. I was the other.

In years past, a woman could only imagine a life at sea as she watched her father, brother, son or her husband disappear over the horizon and turned back towards her home to continue her life without them. But was it any better for the men? I glanced down at my book.

"Ah," cried Captain Harville, in a tone of strong feeling, "if I could make you comprehend what a man suffers when he takes a last look at his wife and children, and watches the boat he has sent them off in, as long as it is in sight, and then turns away and says, 'God knows whether we ever meet again!'"

It became commonplace for me to be interrupted in my reading. My plastic chair became the therapist's chair, and the bridge deck the patient's couch. Other chairs appeared from nowhere. Sometimes a little queue formed, not in a line but as shadows lurking behind bulkheads until I became free for them to approach. Then the process would begin all over again. Rarely was I asked a question. I was there to listen. *A woman is programmed to listen. Isn't she?*

The Major was exempt from these therapy sessions; he never seemed to need an ear to listen to him; he was fine just the way things were. And Rob was too preoccupied with his responsibilities to talk about himself; he was concentrating on the task at hand. He had been expecting me to complain about my basic accommodation and life on board in general, but to every enquiry about my well-being, I answered that all was good: the food, the cabin, the men's language. He seemed relieved, and with a sensitivity I was not expecting from an ex-marine, he showed me a washing machine hidden in a cupboard that I could use if I didn't want to give *all* my clothes to the laundry man.

Unexpectedly, Jean Roux called another meeting in the conference room, so I tagged along with my camera. He was as pale and serious as ever, his body language exuding his powerful, quiet air of authority. His decision-making commanded respect without him ever raising his voice, and I thought how different he was from some of the other men. Only the day before, I had observed Tom, the Major's sidekick, giving an order so precise and clipped to a little Indonesian worker that he froze in his shoes, unable to respond.

Jean Roux waited for us all to settle. He tolerated my being there, but I was aware that he would have preferred it if the meeting was not exposed to my prying lens. Pierre Valdy was particularly quiet, but then Jean Roux signalled him to speak.

"Zer has been, how do you say? A mis'ap," he said gravely. *A mishap?*

He had to admit that the basket had inadvertently been tipped on its side by the grab. There was some ironic laughter, but Pierre contended that these things happen when you are working with untried technology.

The manoeuvring of the grab resumed, and the atmosphere in the mess was still intimidating. It acted like a wall between the men and me, and so I would eat quickly and leave them to unwind in their own company. I assumed I made them feel inhibited, for they wanted to talk about women in an unrealistic way or brag about something I would instinctively know was not true. Whatever it was, my presence clearly disturbed them. The jokes were guarded, except from Major Hopps, who continued to swear and cuss in front of me as if I were one of the troops, much to my approval.

One day, Rob joined us. Half-way through yet another curry, he turned to me and asked what working in television was like.

"Well, for a start, it is run by a bunch of cunts," I replied.

There was a moment's silence all around the room, then a smile flickered across Rob's face. The Major's eyes twinkled; he beamed at me, and I carried on eating. From that day on, I was welcomed into the mess. The swearing belted out in abundance, and I was present when news and rumours circulated, for the mess was the beating heart of the ship. I spent more and more time there. Not only was it the only place to eat but it was also where everybody congregated when the cabins became too hot and the isolation too much.

The cook would personally deliver my plate of food to me while his staff called out different versions of my name. And it was while I was having breakfast, which consisted of a plate of chopped sausages and cold potatoes (mealtimes never coincided with the clocks but worked to shifts), that Captain Paul circulated a rather alarming missive.

Chapter Nineteen

As he handed me the letter, the Major commented that, as usual, the Captain was a little late in the day. I read a command not to disclose where we are. "How," I said, "could we do that?" I was unsure of what the problem was.

Rob visibly tensed up for a moment, and a stillness came over him. "Our position has been leaked by somebody on board using the satellite phone," he said, lowering his voice. "I have a hunch who that might be."

"Who?" I asked. But Rob wouldn't be drawn on the matter.

"We need to be on our guard; that's all."

"On guard against whom?"

"Pirates. Waiting for us to find something."

This was chilling news, although it was quite hard to imagine. We were so far from any shipping lanes, and we had never actually encountered another ship. As I had already experienced, the *Flex LD* was not an easy ship to locate, but once found, we would be a victim of our static position.

"Our remoteness might prove to be our best safeguard from marauding buccaneers," Rob added, sensing my alarm.

When I mentioned this to Brad, he seemed particularly concerned. "Piracy is a threat to be taken very seriously," he told us. "We need to be on the lookout."

But the Major, in typical military fashion, seemed less bothered.

"No ship is unarmed," he said and winked at me.

In the control room, Al sat motionless, staring at a screen full of sediment. Jean Roux had lifted the grab free, and they were both waiting patiently for the lens to clear.

The sudden cessation of cranking and screeching meant that the grab had reached the wreck. Two hours of surveying would ensue before another grab could be made, then Jean Roux had to decide if the weight of the contents was too low, in which case he would deposit the load into the now-righted seabed skip and wait until it was substantially full enough to bring it to the surface.

Outside, I bumped into Richard, or *Riccardo*, as he had now decided to call himself. He had been banned from the monitor room for causing disruption. I walked swiftly away and scanned the horizon for a pirate ship, but the sea met the sky along the usual line, unbroken.

Is this how you start a production company, looking out for pirates on the high seas? Is this the way to conduct your life – loving someone already married from miles away in the middle of nowhere? At times, I longed for home. But there was only one thing for it now. *I would take my chances with the pirates.*

That night, having lost any sense of when to sleep, I was lying on my bunk grappling with my imagination, which was constantly transporting me to places I didn't want to go. I started to believe I was the only one who would see the pirates coming. I left the solitude of my cabin and went up on deck. My eyes were adjusting to the darkness of the stars after the bright neon lights of the corridors when the silhouette of a man came into focus. He was standing alone, looking intently down over the rail.

When Rob saw me, he called me over. Hundreds of squid, some extremely large and quite sinister in their numbers, were darting in and out of the ship's lights below the waterline like mini submarines. We had seen squid before, but never so many. What was even stranger was that they were accompanied by a number of crabs not normally visible so far from shore. We were often visited by dolphins, sometimes sharks and frequently flying fish that leapt high into the air, reminding us how birds were missing from our lives, but this extraordinary spectacle was not like anything we had witnessed before.

"Strange sight; something must have disturbed them," he said as he turned away. I expected him to return to his cabin to his calculations, but instead he sat with me on the deck above the bridge, where there was a clear view of the floodlit rig in the night sky. We listened to the perpetual screaming of the winch, rotating the pipes first up a notch and then down, constantly turned by the overworked Indonesian drill crew.

With his spiky blonde hair and tanned face, Rob looked handsome in the reflected light. The actor, Maria Aitken, had once given me some advice: "When in the Amazon with a remote tribe, sleep with the chief, then nobody else will bother you," she said. She seemed to know about these things. And Rob was definitely the most powerful man on the ship. But was he ready for an invasion from armed pirates?

"Yes, I'm ready," he said softly, and our conversation continued, addressed to the night sky.

"These stars remind me of the time I spent in this part of the world a long time ago," he said.

"Good memories?"

"Yes. I was serving with the Royal Marine Commandos in Aden."

"Aden?"

"But then I was loaned out to assist in training young Omani recruits. I ended up as commander of the Sultan's Coastal Patrol Dhow because I had the relevant experience and a navigator's ticket."

"Sounds romantic."

"I suppose it was until I was sent back on secondment from the Royal Marines in 1971, when the Dhofar war was in full swing. That's when I fought alongside Gareth." *Gareth.* I must have signalled my displeasure, as Rob was quick to defend him. "He fought like a lion. I'll never forget it."

I, on the other hand, had never fought alongside him. How loyal servicemen are to one another when they have been through combat together. I had no proof that Gareth had switched the boats, but one thing was for sure: *Somebody had switched them.*

"Was it Gareth?"

"What?"

"Who traded our boat for a dhow?"

"I don't think so. Why would he do that?"

"He likes to save money."

"That's true."

"Hervé intimated to me that a palace representative or maybe even you are to blame."

Rob was quite indignant at this suggestion.

"I would never have put your lives in danger," he protested.

"Maybe it was Hervé?" I said.

"Well if he did, it almost backfired on him."

"Was there any concern when we didn't arrive?"

"Yes, of course, I was expecting you in daylight, so by 7 pm, I contacted the Palace Office. But no one there could tell me anything about the boat you had left on, and there was no sign of any of you on shore either. So I arranged for extra lights to be rigged on the derrick for you to see us."

"But we saw nothing."

"That's because you were nowhere near us."

"And never would be without navigation."

"Quite. But we didn't know that, so at 8 pm, I called the Palace Office again, requesting that if there was still no sign of you by 10 pm, could they put a police launch on standby to go in search at first light. Meanwhile, Brian Shoemaker was becoming more and more agitated and wanted to contact the American Fleet for assistance. A row broke out between us because I didn't want the situation to escalate too quickly; I wanted to do things in a systematic way, and besides, there were no U.S. naval vessels in the area. The nearest is a mile and a half below us."

He continued to tell me his side of the story, which I had longed to hear. As the weather worsened, he suspected that we had experienced engine failure and that we were drifting. At 10.30 pm, a driller thought he saw a red rocket flare north-east of the *Flex LD*.

"A red rocket would have been more useful than a gun."

"You never know when you are going to need a gun," Rob said without irony. "I told the Captain to stay in position as you were more likely to see us in the dark rather than us finding you in a small, unlit boat, but then I became increasingly under pressure to go rescue you."

So Rob gave the order to commence recovering the grab from the bottom of the ocean and informed the Society for Sea Rescue in Norway that a flare had been sighted. The instruction from them was to go towards it, which was a dilemma for Rob as it was in the opposite direction from the search he was planning. At one minute to midnight, the palace informed him that a police launch would go look for us. Rob called Gareth, who told him that we were sure to be all right.

"Make men of those lawyers, character building. As for Katie, tough as old boots." *That's a first.*

By dawn, the grab was secured under the derrick, and the *Flex LD* was free to proceed in a box search, the first corner being where the red rocket was last seen. At 6.45 am, Rob sent a message to the British Embassy in Muscat; the reply was that, given time, we were sure to *turn up*. Jean Roux, being French, contacted the French Admiral in Djibouti and told him that our little food-container-throwing Frenchman was on board the supply boat. The French Admiral wasted no time scrambling an anti-submarine jet to go look for us. *Remember to always travel with a French national.* But they found nothing and so turned back.

The U.S. Embassy was informed that a rescue operation was underway. As the storm intensified, Rob contacted Muscat again, only to be told, "No problem, the Royal Omani Air Force is being mobilised." *No problem.*

Rob made some rough calculations and faxed a chart of areas in which the Omani military aircraft should search, based on the time and direction from where we set off and taking into account the wind that night. Another few hours and he intended to call for American backup, but he wanted to give the Omanis every opportunity first. Although, by now, he was wondering if they had ever received his chart. He was not convinced that any plane had taken off.

No Omani plane took off.

At 8 am, the *Flex LD* turned the first corner of the search box, but there was nothing showing on their radar. They attempted to find out whether we were equipped with a radar reflector. *We were not.*

Nobody could tell Rob anything at all. By midday, the embassies would have to inform our next of kin that we were missing. A tanker was sighted and radioed for assistance, but the call was ignored.

Finally, Rob received word that we had turned up safely in Raysut. The *Flex LD* returned to the site and proceeded to lower the grab. Twenty-four hours of recovery had been lost and at $50,000 a day. No wonder nobody was smiling at us when we finally drew alongside.

"And what about the red rocket?" I asked.

Rob shrugged. "Must have been the Indian fishing boat."

We sat in silence for a while before Rob spoke again.

"Why didn't you turn back earlier?"

"Neither Hervé nor Al wanted to do that."

"I'm surprised. They should have turned back after 12 hours; without an engine, those dhows can go down very fast."

"Can they? Another thing I'm glad I didn't know."

"There must have been a deal between the police and the dhow owner. Someone made some money out of you."

We were cheap.

"Hervé agreed to it. Gareth would have to approve it. As for Henry, 'Oh, there will be frigates and helicopters and royal launches all to hand.'"

Rob laughed. "What would he know?"

For some reason, I was not as angry with Henry as I wanted to be there was something affable about him; I was more angry with myself. Did I really think as a woman I shouldn't speak up, even if it meant going against my own judgement?

"The newspaper *Gulf News* has reported that five men went missing on their way to a *treasure ship*," Rob said, "one Briton, a Frenchman and two Americans. The men had been found by the French military and were in good condition."

"Well, it's good that the men survived."

Rob missed my quip because he was too preoccupied with his thoughts.

"I think we can guess how they got hold of the story. They may as well have radioed all the pirates in the area direct. I really hope the British press hasn't got hold of it."

I hope so, too. Somebody might wonder where I am.

A long silence followed.

"What would you prefer, Rob, if you were lost at sea, to be British, American or French?"

"Well, the French were quick off the mark, and the Americans definitely would have come especially with a government official on board."

The power of AI.

"But the attitude of the British was that they would be fine." "Which I suppose was true," I said, "unless you are a VIP, of course. Then they'd have come."

The power of celebrity.

Here, I was in the Indian Ocean's own empty quarter, with the sweet taste of salt air in my mouth, at a rare time when the elements had decided to leave us alone. The night sky was softly floating on a cool blue sea, encircling our two little chairs on top of the bridge.

As I reflected on my good fortune, Rob misread my silence.

"Are you worried about pirates?"

The men's daring was contagious. I came straight back at him.

"Of course not! I wouldn't want to miss any of the action."

"I hoped you'd say that," he said.

Chapter Twenty

I soon realised that life on a drill ship is not unlike other working merchant vessels, cut off from the world by a mass of water and dependent on the weather. The steel grid walkways are covered in inches of grease, and the distinct smell of diesel, blended with curry, is never far away. Time is of absolutely no consequence; days and nights are all one and the same, only broken by mealtimes. Men are either working or resting; there are no mornings, afternoons or evenings, just shifts.

The decks continually move beneath your feet as the swell lifts the ship in all directions. Metal doors slam day and night, the engines grind, the rig scrapes and strains, lifeboat tarpaulins flap, and somewhere down below someone is practising their karaoke. Of course, sailing ships are quieter, if you can ever find one where the music is turned off; you can listen exclusively to the sounds of canvas sails and creaking wood, but a drill ship is all noise and smells and routine. My routine was waiting for something to film and looking out for pirates.

There was a time when seafarers would make their own entertainment, play instruments and dance, carve model ships out of wood and paint them, spend time together. But for the below-deck crew, *the roughnecks* as Brad called them, time off involved a lot of DVDs, mainly badly pirated copies that were passed around like currency; a film that had not been seen several times before was at a premium and rare. They were mostly action thrillers. *Actually, entirely action thrillers.* DVD players were cheap to pick up in ports, and after finishing a fourteen-hour shift, the crew tended to disappear with their DVDs to their living quarters and their bunk. *Bunks are private.*

Crew from the Philippines work for very little money and can be found on just about any ship in the world, as they are not protected by unions. They earn in a month what other workers on board earn in a day and send their wages home to their families at every opportunity. They are recruited and supplied by unregulated agencies and tend to be good seafarers, conscientious and adept at giving good service, whether cooking, cleaning or in the laundry or engine room.

Maintenance goes on day and night on board a ship, and you are never far away from the smell of wet paint. There is a reason it is called a working ship. Everyone has a role to play, or they would not be allowed on board. And that included me. I was one of them now.

The drill room was an alternative to the mess when the sun had gone down and the breeze outside was a little cooler. I was now bold enough to march in and join the party, and I was invited into a poker game, which was being played for toothpicks.

After one game with Wayne, I ended up possessing a large pile of toothpicks, much to the Major's enjoyment. Jokes always helped to dissipate hidden anxiety, so there were a few *walk the plank* quips thrown in. Mac was discussing politics with Eric, who saw the world from his own perspective. Of course, he was frequently universally mocked for his *if it ain't Dutch, it ain't much* remarks. The mocking of each other's countries was never ending in some form or other. When Eric scoffed that the British were always the first to a fight, the Major grinned proudly as if he had just been given the best compliment ever. As far as he was concerned, the Brits were superior and did not countenance their natural hierarchy being challenged. The French have a different idea about the pecking order, but their English was limited, so they did not enter into the backchat and consequently were not considered players. Even Brad joined in more, taking part in some crude repartee. He was mostly outwitted by the Major, who loved to provoke him with a dirty joke and a rugby song. Mac supported Brad, his fellow American, with a U.S. Navy ballad in an attempt to out-dirty the Brits, while the French, slightly missing the point, joined in singing the Marseillaise, causing the men from Holland to burst loudly into a song in Dutch while we all looked on blankly.

Brad tended only to talk to me, or at least tease me, when there were other men around him. I supposed that there was safety in numbers. But I was determined to win him over.

I was now included in the banter as the talk increasingly turned to sex and women. I was curious if they thought they had to refrain from such talk when I came on board but no longer felt the need to. *Should I take this as a compliment?*

Or perhaps it was that the more days we were at sea, the more deprivation of sex was preying on their minds. There were many references to what would be their first activity when they went ashore. This talk was amusing but a little unrealistic, as going ashore is not exactly as depicted in old movies. Often there is only a heap of containers miles from the nearest town, or if the port is anything like Mirbat, there is just an empty hotel with a few Swedish dancers lurking in the bar. Brad was particularly keen to get his hands on them. A woman talking to him made him feel uncomfortable, but with a woman stripping, he was in his element. He boasted that he had been married five times and had had many women in his life, sex and women were his favourite subjects. He had earned large amounts of money, which he swore he spent on his mother, his sister and his wives.

"What will you do, Brad, when you finally hang up your cowboy boots?"

"I'm never going to hang 'em up. But when I get away from this can of shit, I'm going to use the dough to find myself a sixth wife."

"Like Henry the VIII."

"Who?"

"English king."

"Yes. That's me, a Texan king. I will buy me a Cadillac and wear my Stetson to my local bar."

Brad had served in the Vietnam War, and his nomadic life had led him all over the world. He liked to brag that wherever he went, he taught those under him how to make Irish coffees just the way he liked them. He also expected everything to be clean and tidy. Rob told me that Brad spent days scrubbing his cabin before he would lay out his belongings neatly inside. How he managed to work in Angola, which he described as *hell on earth*, was anyone's guess.

"I had to tape over the bullet holes in my office every morning, but I could name my fee because nobody else would work there. Made a lotta bucks."

He had survived three helicopter crashes, telling me that some of the Asian ones *were not too hot on maintenance; often the mechanics and pilots were drunk*. Once, he held on to a tail rotor in the China Sea for four hours before he was picked up.

"Wow, that must have been hairy."

"Yeah, and by the time they got to me, I was sober too."

And yet he was accountable for the whole recovery operation. In between the boasting and the innuendos, I could sometimes see the responsibility weighing down on his shoulders as he made his way to his ultra tidy cabin at night.

I bumped into him one afternoon on the boat deck next to the accommodation block. He had just discovered the door on one of the lifeboats had been so well painted that it could not be opened. He asked me if I knew where my life station was and which lifeboat I should go to. *Of course I know*.

"Number Five," I replied.

"And do you know what to take with you?"

"Yes, my clothes if you are going to be in the same one." He loved this and laughed approvingly.

Ever since my whole being had been tossed in the air by the dhow, fragments of the past had landed all over my cabin. I was frequently in there, trying to pick them up and put them back together. *Had I literally run away to sea?* The same refrain over and over. Either way, my heart was not still. I knew what it was to love but not openly. My personal life was much more complicated than a bunch of men chasing after silver. And yet here I was masking again, flirting, untrue to myself. But just like the men, my deepest thoughts were private, and, like them, I was living a phoney existence, and that can drive you to do all kinds of crazy things. So many secrets on this ship. Who could I ever share mine with?

Nobody.

Chapter Twenty-One

A sudden listing of the entire ship threw me out of my bunk. I reached for my camera and ran up the metal staircase to the meeting room.

What everyone had been dreading finally happened. The DPS, which was supposed to keep the *Flex LD* within five metres of its station, failed to self-adjust. Instead of compensating for the heave of the waves and holding the ship in position, the *Flex LD* shot five hundred metres to starboard. If the grab had snagged on the wreck when the recovery ship took off like that, it could have been disastrous. The strain on the drill string would act like a gigantic rubber band, breaking the pipe and backlashing onto the men on the platform.

Jean Roux pronounced that the whole operation could be lost if the pipe were to break. "I refuse to go deeper into the holds unless something is done about this lurching tub of shit they call a ship."

Fortunately, when the *Flex LD* took off, the grab was hovering above the SS *John Barry* and swung across, clearing the wreck before ploughing into an undulating seabed.

Behind the bravura, Brad was genuinely concerned about his men and their safety at sea. He was always looking out for them. He considered that generally the breaking of international law stemmed from a high seas attitude because no one would ever know the outcome. His men were operating extremely dangerous machinery, and they were using metal grinders with no protection.

"What I want to know is why there is no medic or medical equipment on board?" he said forcefully to nobody in particular in the emergency whiteboard meeting that had been called. Heads were bowed, and the floor was scrupulously studied. There seemed to be an obvious answer to me. *Sacrificing lives for the sake of money.*

Even though some wag had written *Hot Lips* on my door, I knew only too well about the lack of medical personnel and supplies, for I slept in a cabin every night with what little there was. And we certainly were not in helicopter range, not from land anyway.

We had entered some other world with its own laws.

Men can do what they want at sea and do not have to pay the price for their actions. A wife disappears overboard on an around-the-world yachting holiday. Stowaways on container ships have been known to be tossed overboard to save the captain from having to turn them in on reaching port. Female crewmembers have reported incidents of rape without recourse. It has been going on for centuries: a cabin boy was lucky if his captain turned out to be a good man. But as a stationary ship, we were faced with private dangers.

The crisis meeting developed into a heated one. No one seemed to notice me filming. There was the continuing consternation from Pierre and Jean Roux about the DPS, but Captain Paul did not seem unduly worried. He gabbled on in French to his compatriots until Rob insisted he speak in English.

"The mechanism 'as only partly failed."

"Partly failed! That means it has failed," said Jean Roux, who could not conceal his fury.

"*Non, non au contraire*, the zystem is perfectly adequate for an operation inside a ten-metre box, but when lowering fifty tonnes of steel through a 'atch, we need more precision."

Now Pierre was incensed.

"The grab is perfectly balanced—" but the Captain interrupted his protestations while the first mate translated.

"We are limited to two satellites, which are splitting the averages in holding our position. Three satellites would have been better."

"Having three is only available to the military," Rob interjected.

"Exactly," agreed the Captain, "so we are using a third reference point, an acoustic one." He paused. "Unfortunately, this is the element that failed," he added reluctantly.

An operation on this scale had never before been achieved, and the reality was that the technology was still fairly primitive and required a lot of creative thinking. Two years earlier, a famous treasure hunter, Keith Jessop, had been commissioned to search for the exact location of the SS *John Barry*. Pierre had been on the survey ship with him, and once pinpointed, he had been down to the wreck in the Ifremer submersible. He thought he could blow open the holds with a large amount of explosives, but the *John Barry* was having none of it. Even as the survey boat vibrated above with the shock waves bouncing off the ocean floor, the explosives had no effect. Down below, a defiant Liberty ship lay undisturbed.

Pierre returned to France and spent the next eighteen months designing his masterwork, so he refused now to be held responsible for keeping the recovery ship in place.

Jean Roux agreed. He asserted, in no uncertain terms, that something had to be done about the situation.

"A DPS expert must be sent for, or we abandon the whole fucking thing." And with that demand, he resolutely left the room.

Captain Paul was visibly downcast at this suggestion, and the meeting dwindled into an atmosphere of reflection threaded with despair.

"Well, that's never gonna happen," said Brad as he too left the assembly of tired drill workers, who were once again wondering how they had become pioneers in the unfamiliar world of treasure hunting.

A vast, ominous shadow on the sea, cast by black clouds shielding the sun, signalled that a storm was coming. Being high up on deck and not in a fishing dhow was of little comfort. Stores were running low, but the arrival day of a phantom supply boat came and went. I had requested more tapes for the camera, but that was pretty low on the list, although a little more hopeful than a DPS expert materialising from nowhere. Apparently, a patrol boat had set off from Oman but turned back because of the impending weather, so nobody was leaving our ship, not yet anyway. Not such good news for a Filipino mechanic who had recently come out in a body-covering rash. That night, we discovered another crewmember had also developed a rash that no one could explain.

Brad again expressed his view about the lack of a medic on board.

"They think that because we won't have a blowout like you might encounter on an oil rig, we are not in danger. They are fucking crazy."

"Crazy," Wayne agreed. "Always trying to save the ship's company money. They're as tight as the bark on a gum tree."

The dhow and the police launch flashed in my mind.

Somebody switched them.

We were given the news that there was a French Navy frigate *passing* and their doctor might be able to visit our spotty men. This seemed a bit unlikely, as Filipinos are not usually considered that valuable. It was more likely that the

French Navy was showing an interest in us. It was well known that Jean Roux had *connections* with them, but nobody could verify what they were.

The rumour was that the French had lost one of their submarines and were interested in a device that could retrieve them at such depths. Whether any of this was true or not, I had no means of knowing, but there was no doubt that the result of our endeavours would prove to be significant for the military in any future underwater recoveries.

Sure enough, a French warship was heading straight towards us. On the helideck, Jean Roux, with his bleached skin as pale as his grey and white hair, made a rare appearance outside. He hardly ever spoke to me, but he did now.

"No filming. Put that camera away."

The frigate was about six miles off our starboard side when a helicopter took off and made its way towards us. It settled hesitantly onto our helipad, and two men dressed in immaculate white shorts, long socks and white shirts, complete with gold epaulettes, stepped onto the *Flex LD*. Here was the admiral of the Indian Ocean's French Fleet and his second in command.

Jean Roux greeted them without introducing Rob or any of his men. They went straight to a closed cabin. It was strange to see an actual helicopter on the usually deserted helideck, its blades turning slowly as the pilot waited patiently. Spying me, he looked both surprised and amused, so I waved, and he waved back.

Twenty minutes later, the two men in white re-emerged, and the helicopter lifted off as stealthily as it had arrived. For a few seconds, it hung detached in the air, nose down, above our crew of dirty overalls. Then, like some giant metallic insect, it soared away. Seconds later, it was reduced to the size of a bee, buzzing towards its hive in the direction of the setting sun.

Apparently, the admiral had brought croissants from their ship's bakery for the men on the bridge and red wine for Captain Paul.

The sick mechanics remained unattended.

Too hot to be in my hospital cabin and too hot to be on deck, there was no other choice than to go to the cool of the mess. I was received with the cries of *Katarina, Katarina* from the galley. *A woman's name is hard to remember.*

Rob was angry he had not been introduced to the admiral. It had been a solely French affair. The Major decided to change the subject and lighten the darkening mood by keeping the present company entertained. While savouring his one and only cool beer, he extrapolated on the rules of cricket to Mac. In no time at all, Mac was completely confused, trying to follow his animated monologue, which started with him drawing a circle, calling it the cricket square, before going on to describe a silly point, a cow corner, a third slip and a gully. The more lost his audience became, the more the Major enjoyed the sound of his own voice. He pressed on, stifling any interjections from his baffled but intrigued listeners. He explained, at some length, all the different scenarios that can take place in a test match. He was meticulously building up to the climax, which he coolly delivered: "And after five days, it usually ends in a draw." This outcome was hailed with hoots of derision. Judging from the expression of extreme satisfaction on his face, this was just as the Major had hoped.

"It's no wonder cricket has never caught on in the States," Mac said.

Feigning surprise at this remark, the Major's bright eyes twinkled and his mouth curled up at the corners before he broke into a hearty laugh, looking at me as his audience peeled away, leaving us alone together.

"How can you not get cricket?" he said. "Greatest game in the world, invented by us, of course."

"So, what's next for you?" I asked.

"Colombia," he said. "Negotiating with kidnappers can be very lucrative."

"Do you ever have to pay up?"

"Never." He chuckled.

The conversation found its way to his tours of Northern Ireland and how humour carried him through when diffusing a bomb.

"We always saved the best jokes for the hairiest moments. My closest friend and fellow soldier was blown to pieces de-wiring a nail bomb, and that night, our squad nailed signs to his bedroom door saying, *Good Riddance* and pictures of scattered body parts."

"But why?"

"Because we loved him; he was one of the best," the Major said without hesitation.

"And if I am shot by pirates, what will you write on the door of my disused infirmary?"

He winked at me.

"I'm afraid you will never know," he said.

Chapter Twenty-Two

The cyclone season was now closing in on us, and the weather was beginning to deteriorate. Our weather window had shrunk to a matter of weeks, maybe even days if the sea started to rough up. But we couldn't go back with nothing – no silver coins, no bullion. *Could we?* I was beginning to see what the networks had meant about filming a salvage operation. A treasure hunt was all or nothing.

"What if they don't find it?" the commissioning editors had said. They weren't going to risk funding a film crew with nothing to show. I had resented their cowardice, but now I was beginning to see that they may have had a point. On board our ship, nobody cared whether a film was delivered or not; they cared that the whole operation was at stake. What had started out as a sure-fire recovery, with all the bravado and confidence of a warrior going into battle, was beginning to shred and fizzle and was bordering on panic. Tempers tazered across the white room. The time to speculate as to what was lurking in our beloved wreck was running out. The measured discussions of old were turning electric and irrational.

"Forget the coins, let's go after the bullion," Riccardo shouted.

"What bullion?" said Rob seething.

"Oh, come on, you know it's there; you think we don't know?"

Riccardo was convinced that Hold Number One contained the silver bars, although they could as easily have been loaded into Hold Number Four in the stern of the ship, which lay separately on the sea floor. Nobody knew. But what we did know was that coin boxes had been identified and were in reach. A heated exchange ensued about whether to continue in Hold Two or smash through to the adjacent Hold Number One and go for the bigger prize.

The normally calm Rob was the most vexed by Richard's outburst. The unthinkable for him was to alter direction and sabotage the mission. He was a man who wanted proof, not dreams. His remit was to return with the coins, and he was determined not to lose them by making a dash for the mythological bullion. His methodical approach so far had led them to the right deck where the coins were stored; it was just a question now of salvaging them. He took a deep breath.

"We have seen the wood from the coin boxes, and they could be on the tween deck above Two; to get to Hold One means tearing the tween decks apart and risk losing the coins. We are not going to risk it. Now everyone, go back to your stations; we have work to do."

At this command, Riccardo stormed out, trying to bang the metal door behind him, but it only swung open again, leaving a gaping doorway. We all stared at it for a moment before Jean Roux added his usual mantra.

"And if we are to succeed in anything, the accuracy of the DP system is critical," he said, looking at Captain Paul, who had been listening quietly, the ever-deepening lines on his face betraying his anguish. The responsibility of sustaining our position fell squarely on his shoulders.

The operator dumped another grab load onto the skip on the seabed, and then Jean Roux ordered him to stop. He was concerned that it was becoming extremely heavy and needed to be retrieved before the heavy seas made the manoeuvre impossible. The grab hooked onto its handle and began the long journey back to the *Flex LD*.

From 8 pm onwards, we were on the rig watching as the skip tried to emerge trapped in the vice of the grab's jaws. Inch by inch, it scraped through the moon pool with only a few inches to spare.

With tonnes of machinery sloshing about, one of the Dutch men bravely dived in and swam beneath the hull to connect steel ropes to the skip. Brad swung like an orangutan, one arm above his head holding onto his harness, the other hand connecting lines as the skip rasped and screamed at us with the strain of the weight inside. As I filmed, I longed for the diver to finish his work before he was crushed into a pulp.

It was a further three hours before the steel skip was finally winched onto the deck. The diver surfaced from beneath it, swinging precariously above the pool. I was relieved to see him clamber out. The stench of the deep was overpowering, but the workers wasted no time leaping inside; they flung out spanners, valves, a pickaxe with the wooden handle long gone and rotten wood. Always the smell of black, stinking wood. But Rob's decision was vindicated. As the debris was tossed aside there, under some steaming planks, Rob picked out a piece of timber and held it up to the platform above.

"Wood?" Richard called out. "What's to get excited about?"

But Rob ignored him and turned to Jean Roux, who had joined him.

"Not just wood," said Rob calmly. "It's the side of a strongbox, and you can definitely make out the word *Dhahran*. See the holes where the coins have been embedded."

"Interesting," said Jean Roux, taking the wood and studying it.

"Proof that the strongroom isn't in Hold Two after all; they must have installed it above on the tween deck. I wasn't expecting that."

Jean Roux nodded; he wasn't either. He gave the order to descend immediately; there was no time to be lost.

"But we need to go gently," Rob warned. "If we smash through that deck, we will lose them, and it will take a lot longer scooping them up from the hold below."

"Yes, but I cannot hold this ship in situ; they need to be a lot more vigilant up on the bridge," he said, scowling, unable to enjoy the moment while he was still angry with the Captain.

Before the grab could descend onto the seabed, there was the almighty task of hanging the skip inside the moon pool. To enable this manoeuvre, Brad once again needed to attach steel cables beneath twenty tonnes of the suspended *basket*, as the skip was often called. We watched as it slowly disappeared into the deep.

By the afternoon, with the DPS still playing up, Eric managed to lower the grab inside the SS *John Barry*, completely unsighted. But for eight hours, water had to be pumped down the pipe in an attempt to clear the silt that was blocking the camera lens. Making the right decisions was crucial if they were going to progress. Visibility was so poor that there was more debate as to the best course of action.

"It might be quicker to bring the whole bloody mechanism up and clean it on deck," Eric suggested.

"Too late now," Rob said. "We're almost done."

Either way, eight valuable hours were lost.

While the sediment swirled in the monitor, Eric expertly found his way to the tween deck above Hold Two. We looked on. Would we finally see treasure?

The screen began to clear, and the sparkling sight of silver coins came into view before disappearing again in a cloud of clay. Eric snatched at them urgently, as though they would never be seen again if he did not move quickly. Rob and

Jean Roux were for a moment paralysed; the riches inside the grab were staring back at us.

Eric had bagged a grab-load of coins.

"Shall we surface? Or deposit them in the basket?" Rob asked once he had registered what he was seeing.

"Time is of the essence now," Jean Roux replied.

"You're right; it will take too many days to go back and forth; let's use the skip." And the decision was made. Four loads of coins were unloaded into the basket to save time, approximately three tonnes of silver, and the long ascent to deliver the prize began.

I went to my bunk and checked my tape stock. Maybe a few days left if I was conservative; it was hard to tell. Anticipation can destroy sleep just as skulking about behind a wall of pretence at home so often destroyed mine, but this was different. I was alive to the collective excitement emanating from the men around me. And then there was the added tinge of schadenfreude at the prospect of going back to the networks and confronting them with our success against all the odds of weather, time, history, technology, rights and investment. *How satisfying that will be.*

At 4 am, I was still buzzing with expectation, even though it would be several more hours before our sea monster was levered out of the ocean. I checked my camera again, thanking Wayne for the hundredth time under my breath.

The black, churning waves were spiked with white froth; the wind whistled between the decks, and the current threw the ship in all directions, so it was a mystery why the moon pool had turned a transparent aquamarine colour, a complete contrast from the dark ocean whipping itself up outside. The pool was the clearest I had ever seen it.

I followed my daily routine of setting up my camera in the usual place, with the gate open wide enough to capture the chasm below ready to zoom in on the skip when it emerged. The pipes ground and crunched above, lifting, lifting, lifting until the first sighting of the basket was the handle clenched at an angle in the grab. Reluctantly, it kept coming and, before the whole skip was revealed, out poked the barrel of a gun.

"What the fuck?" said Jean Roux. Rob was staring at it too.

"How the fuck did that get there?"

The Major came over to where I was filming. The grab paused and hovered just above the pool with the gun aiming directly at us.

"It's a four-inch deck gun, one that Liberty ships used to defend themselves against surfaced submarines."

"OK," I said. "That's interesting."

"Very," he replied.

A diver swam precariously in the moon pool, beneath the fifty tonnes of swaying metal, and attached steel ropes to the skip so that the grab could be released and a crane take over. Once again, I caught my breath. I longed for him to hurry and be out of there. It seemed that these men were forever dangling under bone crushing metal and all the while there was the constant fight with the sea as the ship battled to stay in place.

As the grab opened its jaws to let go of the bar handle, one of the newly attached steel ropes caught in its teeth and was sawn in half. Now only one steel rope was holding the skip. There were shouts as Brad desperately tried to secure it from above, but before anyone could do anything, there was a deafening cracking noise.

The remaining steel rope had snapped in half under the weight, and in a split second, we were staring into an empty, bright blue pool, as if nothing had ever been there. *Gone*.

The skip is gone.

There was a cry, followed by a stunned silence. I continued to film the vacant pool.

Eric, who was standing next to me, spoke quietly. "That's nice; a week's work in there…"

He then, too, fell silent.

I looked up at an inert Rob and Jean Roux standing on the platform above, staring in disbelief. Everyone was completely static, the colour bleached from their faces until someone shouted, "Where is the diver? Have you seen the diver?"

The camera turned cold in my hands. My nerves were struck by little ice picks all over my body. It was some time before anyone could move, and then I became aware of the diver standing next to me peering into the pool. He had swum under the ship and come up a side ladder and was wondering why the skip was no longer hanging there.

"I'm rather pleased to see you," I said. He seemed pleased, if not a bit perplexed.

Without a word, the men disappeared to their quarters. An hour later, I returned to the scene. Brad, pale and shaken, was sitting on a capstan, staring into the abyss. I did not dare approach him, and he did not look up as I dismantled the tripod. Al was looking into the pool, staring at the Eldorado fish nonchalantly swimming as if they were in their own private aquarium. I watched them with him for a while, but all Al could say repeatedly was, "I don't believe they did that."

The mess was a depressing place to be. Everyone agreed that the important thing was that nobody was hurt, the diver had done the sensible thing, but the words were hollow, and the postmortem went on and on. The consensus was that Brad should have attached more metal ropes to such a weight.

Mac came to Brad's defence. "It would have been less heavy without the gun."

"Yes, why was the gun there?" Rob demanded.

The room fell silent.

"My operator saw it just as the basket was due to be hooked up to the grab," Eric said, deciding to come clean. "He thought it would make a great souvenir, so he grabbed it."

Rob was deflated. "It isn't about us. I have investors to answer to."

Brad had not been seen since I last saw him on the capstan. I retired to my cabin to be alone, even though it was over a hundred degrees in the daytime. I lay on my bunk, my shattered thoughts tumbling around me, and found solace in Jane Austen. Not for the first time, I read the penned inscription inside the front cover.

"There could not be an objection. There could be only a most proper alacrity, a most obliging compliance for public view; and smiles reined in and spirits dancing in private rapture."

At dinner, the discussion was still about analysing what had happened that morning. And still no sign of Brad. There was talk of going to look for the missing skip by using the grab as a camera. In an attempt to lift spirits, bets were placed on whether it could be found.

Pierre pointed out that the skip alone cost $25,000.

"Although on the pozitive, zer iz now one less item to return to France."

At least he would save some transportation fees. But it wasn't much of a consolation. Rob estimated that at least four tonnes of coins, some three hundred thousand, were inside the skip; of course many of these would have fallen out on the way down. It was hard to believe that it would ever be found. Nothing goes straight to the bottom in the space of a mile and a half; despite its size, the skip could have drifted in any direction. The men knew that, but they were speculating to compensate for their loss. *Don't say anything. Eat your curry.*

Mac was angry about the gun. "In business, things always go wrong whenever the focus is split," he said. "Going for a gun is not concentrating on the task in hand, which is to go after the silver."

There was much debate as to whether the weight of the gun had caused the steel rope to snap or whether it was just unfortunate that a cable snagged on the teeth of the grab.

I left them arguing. Back in my quarters, my book was, as always, under my pillow.

"She hoped to be wise and reasonable in time; but alas! Alas! She must confess to herself that she was not wise yet."

Jean Roux and Rob finally abandoned their search on the ocean floor. I had been on board for six weeks and we had not salvaged a single coin, even though we had had them within our grasp. With no basket at our disposal, it would be the grab only from now on, which meant the constant winching of pipes against time.

Desperation was beginning to set in. The jovial atmosphere had expired with the loss of the skip, the banter shelved while we waited for the grab to be forced once more inside the wreck. The whole operation was at risk, and this was never more apparent when a rigger's hand became trapped in some machinery. The man was carried groaning to my cabin and left lying on the hospital bed with his finger hanging off while there was an anxious search for some bandages. A French officer arrived from the bridge.

"It will need stitching," he said, not very convincingly. "The chief engineer will know what to do." So the chief engineer was sent for. He arrived carrying a first-aid manual and proceeded to stitch the finger back on while the relevant section of the book was read out to him. He looked over at me. I must have been gawping helplessly because he decided to put me to some use.

"Do you have any painkillers?" he said.

Relieved to escape from my now fully occupied quarters, I went to hunt for some. I was sure Mac would have a selection. On my return, the situation was not improved by the Major's sidekick, Tom, also arriving with a badly cut hand, which he had caught on a shard of metal while sifting through debris. All we needed now was more mysterious rashes to break out amongst the men.

Rob contacted the Palace Office and requested a boat to come and pick up the rigger to take him to a hospital. He returned with the news that the only boat available was a dhow. This produced some ironic mirth. The rigger was a red-headed Scotsman who was pale to begin with, but his face was now white, and his hand was concealed by a bloodstained bandage. Like everyone on board, he knew how long a dhow's journey would take, and he was not keen to leave us.

"Don't worry," said Rob. "If they can find us, then they can find Oman on the way back."

"As long as it isn't Yemen," Wayne chipped in mischievously. The rigger smiled weakly. But beneath Wayne's cheery exterior was an anger that this continual cost-cutting was risking men's lives.

The search for the silver went on beneath us regardless of accidents and rashes. Depicted on the monitor in the control room was a jumble of torn metal surrounded by fragments of wreckage. The operator had been tearing at the top deck, removing steel in large chunks in order to drive the grab further into the wreck. Sometimes the strain on the pipe was so strong that our ship dipped in the water with the tension. The violence in ripping the wreck apart had caused so much sediment that nothing inside the grab was visible. Frustrated at having to wait so long, Jean Roux decided to dump the load and lower the grab to where the coins had previously been located and then waited for the lens to clear.

We were eating in silence when, over a sea of sullen faces, I saw Rob appear at the door holding his thumbs up and grinning. And then he said what everyone had been waiting to hear.

"Coins in the grab!"

Chapter Twenty-Three

Seizing my camera, I ran with Rob to the control room. Sure enough, there on the monitor, as though waiting for our approval, was what everyone had toiled day and night for: thousands of perfectly round silver coins clenched firmly inside the grab's jaws. Nobody was going to let this bounty get away. *Not this time.*

The air was electric with excitement, the suspense broken by a contained jubilation. Nowhere was it more visible than on the face of Pierre, whose much-criticised design was now proving effective.

Instantly, a meeting was called. We congregated in the white boardroom. Ten hours of hard, tedious labour would follow while the submissive Indonesians on their long shifts, yet again, winched the drill string to the surface one pipe at a time. Everything was at stake now. *Don't fuck up the filming; don't fuck up my new career as a filmmaker.* The crew couldn't afford to fuck up either. The grab held in its jaws the treasure hunters' dreams.

Belief vibrated throughout the ship, making everybody more talkative as we prepared for the grand surfacing. I found a new position between a mass of steel paraphernalia to set up the camera.

At around seven in the evening, more overalls and hard hats than I had ever seen at one time mustered around the moon pool; even Captain Paul and two of his men from the bridge were in unfamiliar positions looking on. Mac and Richard paced around anxiously. Al's face was impassive as usual. Gradually, the monster grab was dragged from the sea. In its dark jaws, gripped with all its might, were some torn-off timbers, but this time we could clearly see the shapes of silver coins glinting like fillings in its teeth, drooling and dribbling seawater and swaying defiantly. Nobody knew what to expect. We all just stared in anticipation.

There was the sound of scraping steel upon steel as a vast metal tray was shunted into position and the grab was winched over it, swinging lifelessly. And then, as though they no longer had the muscle to stay closed, the jaws began to open.

A torrential rain of coins cascaded into the tray and spilled over the deck and kept on. *And on and on.* The grab was vomiting coins like some giant fruit machine whose jackpot was out of control. The long wait of dreams was realised beyond anything anyone had dared imagine.

The roar from the men was drowned out by the sound of teaming coins. No one knew how to react. A kind of mechanical euphoria echoed around the ship.

On and on. Until the last few coins chinked onto the peak of the silver mountain. The grab sighed, exhausted, all its energy spent. For a moment, there was nothing but the sounds of the sea and the whirring of hoists.

Richard suddenly took off around the deck shouting "We're rich," which was hardly true for most of us, especially the crew whose meagre wages were not about to change either.

Mac was beaming. "My, my, it was just waiting to be scooped up."

I did not look up from my viewfinder but kept on turning. An image of the broken camera on Wayne's desk flitted across my memory, and I shook myself into concentrating on the job in hand rather than what might have been. There were no camera phones then, and remarkably, nobody was carrying a camera either. The only record of what was actually taking place was whirring in my hands at that very moment.

Tom leapt into the tray beneath the spent jaws and began to sweep between the teeth. He picked out any remaining fragments using water jets inside and out until he was satisfied that there was nothing left concealed. Each piece of timber was inspected, and many of the coins had to be prized out of the wood before it could be discarded. Even the silt was scrutinised; workers pawed over lumps of white-coloured clay.

A U.S. Marine's boot was given the once-over for coins before it was tossed aside. Finally, the tray was piled high with hosed coins and sat smugly on the deck, splattered with the stinking remnants of the long-forgotten Liberty ship.

The Major barked some commands, and his little team began to shovel spadeful after spadeful of coins into a steel cradle, which when full was hoisted into the *Flex's* hold, which had been empty for so long.

The Captain reappeared carrying bottles of champagne that he must have secreted under his dry command. Smiling and gravelling incomprehensible words of triumph, he popped corks and poured the contents into coffee mugs. We drank in silence, stunned by the enormity of the haul.

Later, a party broke out in the mess and continued into the early hours, but there were no Army Boys to join in the celebration. They, at last, had an assignment to fulfil.

Nobody on board was more relieved than Rob as he announced that, on first reckoning, we had picked up ten boxes of coins. But not content for long, he added the bad news that, with seven hundred and fifty boxes on board the SS *John Barry* and twenty-four hours for each operational grab, we were going to run out of days. As for the chances of reaching the possible location of the mystical silver bullion, which Richard thought would buy him an island in the Caribbean, we could forget about that. Everything was taking longer than anticipated. Once again, optimism had stood in the way of the reality of the size of the operation.

"It is a splendid achievement," Rob admitted almost reluctantly. He could not deny that all those grabs of wood and shredded metal had revealed a treasure chest way beyond his expectations. There would never be any public mention of the coins in the lost skip; that secret was now confined to the deep, quite literally.

Pierre was feeling particularly smug that he had finally proved that his grab could deliver.

"You zee, my invention, there is nothing else like it in all the world."

Even the Dutch had to concede. "Brute force is usually the answer," Eric said, laughing.

Unless, of course, you want to preserve the memory of the Liberty ship's sailors.

Realising that neither Mac nor Richard were present in the mess, I went looking for them. The vertical ladder into the hold was very long. I slung my camera over my shoulder and descended into the dark pit beneath. I admired the men who skipped the rungs and slid down the rails, but this resulted in sore hands red with rust, so I was not about to try. Inside the hold, the metal cradles were being unloaded onto the scales and counted before being deposited into crates.

Mac was very animated. "Welcome to Ali Baba's cave," he shouted to me above the noise of the shovelling. Richard was singing and dancing in front of the workers before throwing himself on top of the coins. This repellent scene made for good filming, and I checked myself for being so disapproving. Surviving the dhow was more important to me than being rich, but then being rich was never something that happened to people who chose a life backstage.

I left Richard still leaping in the way of the men doing the counting. Suddenly feeling exhausted, I clambered up the steel ladder and went back to my airless cabin to number and log the video tapes and charge the camera battery. The atmosphere was stale; the smell of the make-shift surgery hung over the room. I peeled off my overalls and steel-tipped boots; the grime of oil and grease had penetrated my clothes down to my underwear. There was a knock at my unlocked door. I grabbed a towel and opened it to see the cook standing there, grinning.

"You married?"

"Yes," I lied.

"Children?"

"No."

"Why you no children? Your husband no good?"

Difficult one to answer.

"I can give you children."

"No doubt, but not today, thank you."

I closed the door. It had been a long 24 hours.

Chapter Twenty-Four

The next day at breakfast, I discovered that Rob's estimate of ten boxes had been a little on the conservative side.

"Been up all night," the Major hollered at me as he sat down. "Two point five tonnes. That's fifty boxes, 4,000 coins in a box." He grinned as I stared at him, unable to think of a reply.

Eric came in swearing and banged the table with his fist in frustration. "Fucking operating hydraulics inside the module are malfunctioning again."

This latest hitch delayed the grab from descending and caused much frenetic activity around the moon pool. Now that we had found the coins, there was a rush to return to the site before it broke up. Nobody knew how many days we had left – 30 days if we were lucky, but more likely less. The pace was now intense. Everyone concentrated on the task at hand, apart from Richard, who was showing off his latest ryals to various crewmembers.

"That's an awful lot of coins I now own," he boasted spinning a ryal into the air.

"What are you going to do with so many?" I asked.

"Make a great coffee table top, won't they?"

If any of the poor Indonesian workers were found to possess even one coin, they would be flung off the ship, no longer able to send home their pittance of a salary to their families. But Richard, not content with his lot was always apprehensive that someone might end up with more coins than he had.

"Richard is obsessed with treasure," Mac told me. "

"I hope it makes him happy," I answered.

"I doubt it, but it was our quest to find it and that makes us all happy."

To save time, several grabs of cargo had been deposited on one of the decks of the wreck. The process was being carried out blind, as it seemed that the grab had disturbed a cargo of cement bags inside one of the holds. I wondered if this was in fact the secret cargo, not silver bars. But I kept that thought to myself.

The cement at least accounted for the murky vision, making it impossible to see anything other than sediment on the monitor. Again, the operators had to wait for the lens to clear. But given the lack of visibility throughout the process, it was an incredible achievement that there were two tonnes of silver coins already boxed up in the hold.

With little to see, I went up to the helideck to film the sunset. I already had a stock pile of sunsets for cutaways for editing purposes. This one would have to be short. With only one sixty-minute tape left, sunsets were a luxury. What if we did discover the bullion? After the spectacular shower of coins, I could only imagine what a shower of silver bars would look like crashing onto the deck of the *Flex LD*.

And there was Al jogging his way around the perimeter. He stopped when he saw me filming and came over to sit silently down beside me. Our feet dangled over the edge. The sight of the setting sun was nothing new; it took place every evening, but every evening, it still managed to suspend time while we viewed and reflected. We were so far from…well, *everything really.*

To break the silence, I commented on the large haul of coins and the grab's success.

"Yep," he said.

"Al, you either have a very strong bladder or a very strong will. I never saw you move positions on that dhow. Did you never have to use the wonderful facilities?"

"Fine kidneys," he replied. For him, it was a serious question. "And a low intake of fluids." *Fine and stoical.*

"Were you ever concerned, Al? Just a tiny bit?"

"A little. I feel bad that I didn't say anything sooner."

"Well, talking is not your strongest attribute, is it?"

He smiled. "Talking is no good when things go wrong, best to ride it out. But had I known about that rudder…" *Ah, yes, the rudder.* "I noticed the faulty compass when I came aboard and the lack of holes, but that rudder was something else."

"Holes?"

"There should have been holes in the deck for the water to run off." *Anything else?* "And I wasn't happy that the stove slid across the deck attached by a rubber hose to a bottle of methane gas," he continued, more vociferous than I had ever heard him.

I must have missed that one.

"It was bad enough putting out to sea that far with only a single engine but with no safety equipment, radio or navigation…"

He had obviously been mulling things over. After all, he was a U.S. Coastguard; safety at sea was his bag.

"Al, Rob told me about a report that Hervé had written for his company, Trav Ocean. Not surprisingly, our whole dhow incident was glossed over, but what stood out was a revelation I hadn't been expecting."

I was, however, expecting Al to react to this disclosure, but he just stared straight ahead. So I went on.

"I think you should know that in Hervé's report he claimed that the skipper and the owner swore that we were in the right place and that the *Flex LD* had left its position and was no longer where it should have been!" Al sighed a resigned sigh.

"Yeah, the owner told me that too."

Al never mixed much with anyone on the *Flex*; he had the odd technical natter with other officers, but mainly, he kept to his cabin or sat patiently in the control room, quietly watching. Quietly waiting.

"Do you miss home, Al?" I asked him. His expression implied that he had not thought much about it.

"Not really. I miss going hunting with my son in Maine."

I pressed him for a bit more, he said he couldn't live without his children.

"Men and women seldom have the same interests," he said sadly. "I like to go hunting with some of the guys; we stay in a log cabin." *I'd go.*

"Women are interested in shopping and stuff like that."

"Really? I hate shopping."

Al looked at me as if he had just seen me for the first time before turning back to the ocean. We watched the solitary sun disappearing, a flickering red sky was about to put the lights out. It occurred to me that only the overfriendly cook, Cookie, had ever asked me anything about my personal life. Al glanced down at the camera in my lap.

"You make a lot of films?"

My first. "Some."

There was a long silence.

"I've never met an actor."

Worlds apart.

"You live in London?" I nodded.
"What is that like?"
"Well…"

As I struggled to answer his question, he decided to finish our dialogue and stood up.

"I will say this, mate, you handled yourself real well on that dhow, not like those other softies." And with that, he jogged off along the well-trodden perimeter. *I'm his mate.*

I watched him complete another circuit before descending the steel ladder in the dark.

"My idea of good company…is the company of clever, well-informed people, who have a great deal of conversation…"

Richard had become bored; his short attention span was proving the better of him. I assumed that after he'd seen his share of the treasure pour onto the deck, he did not feel the need to repeat the experience, but I was also surprised because of his earlier conviction that there was bullion to be salvaged. Had he lost faith in the operation, or was there something else at play? Whatever the motive, he was in earnest because there was definite talk from him that he might return ashore. Mac hoped he would follow through on this and suggested he go back on the supply boat coming to pick up the mechanic.

"Let's hope he doesn't change his mind," said Mac as he joined Rob and me in a huddle against the rail on the bridge deck. The height and the view provided a good excuse to avoid eye contact, making it a good place for conservation. "We are already receiving a fifth of the spoils; he doesn't need to count any more."

"A fifth? I don't think so," said Rob with surprise. "A hundred coins each is my understanding."

"No, I promise you, a fifth is stipulated in our contract."

Rob recovered enough to say, "All contracts will be honoured, although I do not recall any such agreement being made." But Mac, of course, had his signed piece of paper as evidence.

The morning before Richard, or Riccardo, as he again corrected me, was due to depart, I noticed one of the Indonesians cleaning the remains of a hatch from the SS *John Barry* that Riccardo was taking home to place on his silver coin coffee table. Lying on the main deck on top of his packed suitcase, a ship's laundry bag, was stuffed full of souvenirs for all to see.

Up on the bridge, there were a few jokes about what time the dhow, which was coming to fetch the rigger, would arrive. Seemingly, it had left at 9.30 pm the previous night, but at 10 am, there was still no sign of it. My feet were firmly planted on the bridge deck. *No more dhows for me.*

Incredibly, there was radio contact from the boat. *Radio?* But still, no sign of it on the radar screen. *No reflector, then.*

At 1 pm, the dhow was sighted, but it would be another two hours before they reached us, and by then, it had been 36 hours since the accident.

When it finally arrived, the wooden fishing boat that pitched up and down in the swell was considerably larger than the one I had come to know so well. In fact, it was the largest dhow I had ever seen. It looked seaworthy enough, which I hoped would be of some relief to our departing invalid. However, the waves were too high for it to come alongside us, so the rigger was lowered into a rubber dinghy.

The rigger attempted to wave, but I shouted to him to keep his bloodstained hand above his head. A shark was sighted, and the Major called out, "Yes, don't let any blood go into the water," which brought a lot of laughter from the watching crew and a V-sign from the rigger with his good hand. The dinghy was throwing him all over the place, but the difficult part was climbing up the Jacob's ladder onto the dhow, the side of which was extremely high. As the boat rolled, the ladder swung out as he was halfway up and came crashing back again, smashing his newly sewn-on finger against the beam.

"Ouch," said Wayne. "Good thing he's seeing a doctor."

The dinghy then came back for Richard. The first mate was carrying a large package from the mainland which he threw at the bosun. Rob, Mac and I watched with particular interest as Richard made his way down the *Flex's* slippery ladder to rejoin the outside world. We wanted to make sure he was really going. Once on board, the dhow set off at such a slow speed that they seemed to be rolling and pitching on the spot. Rob's radio crackled, and the dhow's Indian captain's broken voice came through.

"Please, Captain Bob, tell Salalah that we arrive at three in the morning in the night."

Mac and I looked at each other knowingly. At least he had a radio, but neither of us were ever going to disembark this ship until it was safely docked in a port. We'd made that promise to each other in one of our private chats when neither of us could sleep.

"What made him decide to go?" I asked Mac.

"Probably to start suing everyone before I get back," he replied. I tried to resist the urge to laugh. But Mac's dry humour could always make me laugh.

The Major joined us, never one to miss some fun. The four of us started waving furiously. Richard waved back, grinning in a way that only Richard could grin, showing a mouthful of stained teeth. His tousled, uncut hair blew about his face in the wind. Out of earshot, the farewells began.

"Good riddance, my noisy friend."

"Turn him upside down and shake him!" shouted the Major. At this Mac joined in joyfully waving.

"Bye, Riccardo. We'll save you a silver bar."

It was the most jubilant I had ever seen Mac, possibly even more than when the first ryals sprayed across the deck. Mac had long been dismayed by Richard's behaviour. He had been carrying the burden of him since the expedition began, and it hurt. Gareth always referred to them both as *the lawyers*, the dirtiest words in the English language as far as he was concerned, and never by their names. When Richard lived up to Gareth's estimation, Mac had been embarrassed to be associated with him, and yet he was inextricably tied to him. With his departure, the relief was palpable.

A weight as heavy as the grab seemed to lift from Mac's shoulders as the dhow retreated into the twilight. He became more upright and more like a teenager than a man in his thirties. He laughed wholeheartedly with us and waved until the boat was well and truly out of sight.

Several hours later, he was still waving goodbye long into the night.

Chapter Twenty-Five

The package from the dhow contained some newspapers and, more importantly, to me anyway, the one and only Hi-8 tape that existed in Salalah. The tapes I had bought in Camden were now almost full. I had thought of myself as a film director complete with camera and sound, but then I remembered that I had no lights, no spare camera, no decent microphone and I had almost run out of tape stock. When I considered real camera crews, I felt ashamed. The doubts ran and ran in my head, as if I could have done better without the support of a network. *Would a professional only carry one camera, or run out of stock?* My new sixty-minute tape was about to become my most precious possession.

When I arrived at the moonpool, the grab was already discharging seawater and swaying menacingly due to a heavy ground swell and the weight of its load. Clenched in its jaws, embedded in timbers, were more silver coins sparkling in the rising sunlight. Inch by inch, the grab was winched over the deck, where it swung, making a few tantalising gestures before opening its jaws once more, this time to release another five tonnes of silver ryals, many more than had been expected and with a value of roughly a million dollars. Many were stuck in thick white clay from when the grab had hit the mound on the ocean floor and had to be scraped out and separated.

The sifting of the haul into the cradle before it was lowered into the hold took several hours. With very little tape stock left, I became distracted by some sharks swimming off our port side. It took all day for the Army Boys and their team to count and clean the 60,000 coins.

At 3 am, I retired to the mess for a nightcap, but they were serving lamb chops, so I had those instead before descending through a hatch, not dissimilar to something you might find on a submarine, into the bowels of the ship to film the last of the counting and boxing of coins. The weary security men were busy weighing and stuffing coins into sacks, overseen by the ever-cheerful Major, until a sudden explosion followed by a loud hissing sound had everyone scurrying around, unsure whether to leave the coins or stay.

When you see everything through the lens of a camera, you become removed from reality. I hung back, thinking I should film whatever it was that had exploded, until the Major shouted, "Everyone evacuate now!"

One of the workers beat me to the ladder, pushed me aside and scampered up the rungs before me. *Astonishing how fast you can ascend a vertical ladder when you need to.*

The Major followed and was the last man out.

"Well, that wasn't very gentlemanly of him," he said, emerging from the hatch, his eyes twinkling once more in the early morning sunlight.

The counting was delayed while the mystery valve that had blown in the hold was repaired. It was late afternoon on the following day by the time over a100 boxes had been filled.

There was no doubt that information had been leaked, which was hardly surprising given that even our non-English-speaking crew on the dhow had known what we were up to, but news was well and truly out now that we had found the silver. The palace in Oman had been made aware, and Al had been quick to inform the U.S. government, as he was duty-bound, the minute the coins were retrieved. More alarming to Rob was that a press release was giving out details as to the purpose of our mission and claimed that the coins had been sold for $25 each. We were headline news in the newspapers that had arrived on board, but I was trying to suppress the notion that pirates read the papers like everyone else.

For the coins to have already been sold was a bit unlikely, although there was speculation on board that if another Arab prince had promised to help Sheikh Ahmed Farid with the Yemen situation, he may have done some sort of deal with the coins. But Rob very much doubted that there was any such sale; he was more concerned about giving the wrong message to investors, attracting pirates and putting our whole operation in jeopardy. It seemed Sheikh Ahmed was desperate to give a press conference way before time. Rob became quite agitated and frustrated with Henry back in the press office. To stop the leaks, Henry suggested an exclusive.

"He says we need a top journalist from a UK newspaper to report the story."

"How does he propose we do that?" I asked.

"Apparently, he has organised for someone from the *News of the World* to come out here."

"*The News of the World?*" I repeated sniffily. "What, just drop by with his pen and notebook?"

This seemed incredible to me. Here we were in the remotest of locations. Was a reporter from the *News of the World* really going to risk his life on a dhow, even if it was a large one with a radio? Twelve hours of choppy waters. Why was I questioning this so much? Why was I so put out by this news? *My territory to be breached?* When Rob greeted me with the next bulletin, I feigned nonchalance, but not very successfully.

"Henry says he is escorting her." *Her? Another woman.*

"Henry is coming here?"

"Apparently."

"He's got more guts than I thought." I had to admire his determination to be in on the act, although I couldn't quite imagine him squeezing into the latrine on the dhow.

In the mess, the red wine from the French frigate was brought out for Armistice Day, and nobody was resisting. *So not a dry ship after all.* Large tumblers were poured, and there were many jokes of a sexual nature about what the female reporter could expect when she boarded the *Flex LD*.

The jokes were mainly about how she could have at least seventy men in her first hour on board, and given their present state, none of them would take very long.

I should defend her.

I turned to Rob. "Did they talk about me like this before I arrived?" I asked him.

"Oh yes, but then we had to stop when you got here. Since we have discovered you are one of us, we've gone back to our old ways." *I see that now.*

"What is the *News of the World?*" Brad chipped in, crossing his legs to show off his cowboy boots. "I'm not going to be interviewed by anyone, not even you," he said, which was warming in a strange way as it meant he had acknowledged why I was there.

"Just as well, for if they heard your stories, they might forget to mention the silver."

Brad grinned. He was almost back to his old self.

"I can well imagine what you were saying about me before I arrived; sorry if I disappointed you."

"That's OK; it's good to meet a sane woman for a change," he replied.

The British amongst us were hungry for the newspapers that had come on board, and we shared them between us. The chat was mainly about sport, a subject at which I am very adept, much to their surprise. The Femail section of the Mail was tossed towards me by one of the crew.

"Here, some tittle-tattle for you," he called dismissively. "I don't understand it."

"Neither do I," I told him, tossing it back.

It was easy to feel disorientated sometimes, even a little disturbed, when the gender distribution was so imbalanced. I lay in my narrow bunk, comforted by Jane Austen. *"Songs and proverbs, all talk of woman's fickleness. But perhaps you will say these were all written by men."*

I was aware that the noise from the thrusters was different. No longer powering intermittently, I could hear them constantly going all night. The officers on the bridge were hard at work. My alarm was set for 3 am, when the grab was due to surface.

When only nine boxes of coins, each containing four thousand, were retrieved without celebration, I realised how blasé we were becoming. I was more interested in collecting up a few personal items from the wreck, some marine boots and army vehicle parts, which, without Richard there to scoop them up for souvenirs, could be found dotted around the ship.

By 5.45 am, the grab was ready to descend, just as a familiar glow in the sky stole over the flank of the ship. Ever since morning broke on the dhow, I had found the dawn light very reassuring, and I snuck back to my quarters as the sun appeared over the horizon, safe in the knowledge that it would be there for the next twelve hours.

By 1 pm, the cabin was stifling. Lying on the lower bunk, a thought occurred to me: that reporter would soon be in the other bunk. *Bound to be.* Where else could she go?

An unreasonable wave of anxiety came over me, my precious airless space was to be shared with the *News of the World*. But it wasn't only the newspaper she represented that was troubling me, it was the fact that she was a she and I would no longer be the only female on board. I had become used to my unique position amongst the men. I was all confusion. *My status will be diminished.*

Disconcerted, I went looking for some breakfast, but it was lunchtime in the mess and so I had a steak instead. There I discovered the Major describing the British children's TV programme *Blue Peter* to Mac, who was attempting to out-describe him with *Mr Rogers and Hello Neighbour* from the American children's TV series of the eighties. Brad was talking to the first driller about the rigs they had worked on in the North Sea and about the *Piper Alpha* disaster that killed a hundred and sixty-seven people. There were more jokes about the new girl's impending arrival before Rob turned the chat to mountaineering. From disasters, to action, pirates and sex, the conversations lurched like the ship from one wave to another. The Major was now pontificating on how to make a Christmas pudding, his audience perplexed by how long it was before it was eaten.

"Oh yes," said the Major delighted, "leave it for several years; the longer the better!"

He glanced over at me, and his eyes flickered with an idea.

"How about when we get back to port you and me drive from Salalah to Muscat via the Empty Quarter?"

"Quite a long way and a lot of sand."

"Ah, but it would be an adventure, and we could all do with an adventure."

Adventure? When had I been able to resist an adventure? *Well, now, it seems.* I told him I would think about it and retreated to my chair on the monkey island.

The next time the grab surfaced in the moonpool, its jaws were slightly open due to some steel decking tangled in its teeth. The number of coins was disappointing as many may have fallen out on its long journey from the wreck. The only ones inside were stuck to the walls of the grab and were black with marine engine oil. It seemed we had broken into a fuel tank, but we had also found where they kept their spare parts. Spark plugs still in their boxes, valves, pistons all thick with oil dropped into the tray. The smell was overpowering, and the few coins that were recovered were going to need copious washing to restore them.

"Now is the time to go after the bullion," Mac announced.

"Maybe," said Rob. "But we would be ripping the ship apart with no real direction as to where to look. It is not in Hold Two, that's for sure. There is not much left of that."

The following morning, Rob appeared, by his standards, almost excited. He had been thinking all night and had come up with an idea that might save a lot of time. Instead of probing holds for bullion, why not break into Captain Ellerwald's cabin on the SS *John Barry* and grab the safe? Inside were bound to be the documents regarding the cargo. This seemed a brilliant idea to me. Rob had been studying his Liberty ship plans so as to work out where in the captain's cabin the safe might be. As he was telling me this, he was called to the bridge, and I ran after him. There was an oncoming vessel on the radar screen approaching at twenty-five knots.

Chapter Twenty-Six

Mac could hardly contain himself when he saw Henry was arriving on an Omani destroyer equipped with fore and aft Exocet missiles, anti-aircraft guns, a helicopter and at least sixty sailors. The warship was gliding towards us at top speed, cutting through the water without a pitch or a roll. The first figure to come into focus in my lens was Henry, dressed in immaculate, tight-fitting white, standing aloft on the gun deck. As the warship drew closer, he was shouting orders at us that nobody could hear above the noise.

Rob laughed. "I think he's calling for us to shut the thrusters down so that they can draw alongside." *As if.*

To add insult to injury, we didn't even have to lower a Jacob's ladder; a gangplank was produced.

"There will be a red carpet next," said an incredulous Mac, sighing.

Proof that Henry does have the ear of the palace was now confirmed by the method by which he arrived. He was the first across the gangplank, followed by Annette, *The News of the World* reporter, who was actually wearing high heels and a skirt. Behind her was a very unsteady photographer who was green with seasickness. The injured Scottish rigger was next, complete with a properly strapped-up hand and a haircut so neat that we did not recognise him at first. Henry was talking nineteen to the dozen to Annette pointing to the rig and describing how the treasure was retrieved. She did not appear to be listening, I suppose because she had been travelling with Henry long enough. To my amazement, she made a direct line for me.

"There you are, surrounded by *so* many men! And you witnessed all this with your own eyes?"

"Well, mainly through the viewfinder of my camera, but yes. Yes, I did," I said, surprising myself.

I tried to introduce her to the crew looking on, but she cut me off and whispered that she only wanted to talk to Brits.

"Oh, in that case, you should meet the Major; he is in the hold, counting coins."

"Excellent. Take me there."

I led her to the hold where the coins were stored and descended the long, rusty ladder down into the pit. When I got to the bottom, I looked up to see that she was still there, peering through the hatch.

"Are you coming?" I called.

"No, too steep for me," she yelled. So I came back up.

"Well, anyway, they're down there," I told her.

There then followed a whirlwind tour of the ship. But Annette wasn't very interested in logistics or machinery.

"So tell me, so many men to fancy, who have you shacked up with?"

"Uh, well…Would you like to see the control room?"

"I think the real story is *you*. You with the pick of all these men. I wish I could stay longer."

"I do have another bunk in my cabin for you," I said.

She looked at me as if I had just spoken in a discontinued language.

"You mean you are not in the captain's?" She winked.

"There is something I would like you to report in your newspaper."

"Yes, what is that?" she asked, suddenly intrigued.

"My journey here. Somebody switched a launch to a dhow and…"

Henry was calling out as he rushed across the deck and bulked his way between us.

"You need to get Rob to search Hold Number One; that is where the silver bullion is. I'm sure of it. It actually belonged to Stalin, you know."

"No, I didn't know," I said. Although why he thought that, I had no idea.

"You must not waste any more time. Get into Hold One!" he ordered, as if I were in charge of such things. I looked to see if Annette was taking notes, but she was now drifting off as she has spied Tom standing nearby.

"How are you, Henry? Are you well?" I enquired, trying to steady the conversation. "Yes, never better. I have a message from Gareth; he says if you have the footage of the coins, you no longer need to stay as they are no longer funding you."

"Oh? I wasn't aware I was being funded."

"This documentary film you are making has got to make money. Everything is costing so much."

"Well, please tell Gareth I promise not to cost another penny."

I had no intention of returning to Oman on anything other than the *Flex LD* and certainly not on Henry's warship. I could not imagine I was costing anyone very much. I was not even using my one beer a day quota.

Before I had the chance to dwell on this memo from Gareth, the Major, who had appeared from the hold to see what all the fuss was about regarding *the other* woman on board, grabbed me by the arm.

"Come on, let's go aboard the destroyer and explore," he said.

I duly followed him, leaving Henry to point out all the unique features of the *Flex LD* to our roving reporter.

The Major and I enjoyed prancing across a gang plank. It was as though we had escaped a prison ship and found one not tied to the seabed. He was ecstatic when he realised it was British-made and eulogised about the guided missile launchers and the anti-aircraft guns.

"You like guns, don't you, David?"

"Love them," he replied. "Never happier than in the company of a lethal weapon."

Such a winning grin.

"Have you always loved them?"

"Always." His eyes sparkled with boyish delight.

Back on the *Flex LD*, Annette was busy interviewing Rob while Henry prompted him. Rob was not one for exaggerating his achievements, and he was particularly wary about the consequences of our story being broken to the world. There was nothing he could do about it now. It would be front-page news on Sunday.

I attempted to speak to Annette again to tell my story, but Henry acted as a human shield. The photographer took pictures of the coins in the hold, but in my cabin was the tiny tape that held the moment when thousands of coins cascaded over the deck; I was not about to hand that over to anybody. Yet having been so irked at the thought of another woman on board *my* ship, I now had the unnerving experience of not wanting her to leave. Evidently, we were very different women, but I hadn't had any female company for a while now and felt ashamed to think I had felt so threatened by her presence. She had as much right as I had, and yet I had become extremely possessive of the *Flex LD* and her men. Before she left, she flung her arms around me, the warm scent of female flesh pressed against me, transporting me back to the land I once knew, and with a wave, she was gone.

We watched the warship speed away as fast as it had arrived, taking Henry and Annette and her chronicle with them. A curious sense of sadness washed over me, tainted with relief. I looked around at the men staring over the rail as if they had just been visited by an apparition, which in a way they had. One they could see but could not touch. We slowly returned to our quarters. When your world shrinks, you stay close to your own.

The daily rhythm of the working day had been disrupted by the lightning visit from the warship. It was a day or two before things returned to normal. It was as if we had been invaded and plundered and left to make sense of it all. Not by pirates but by the outside world. At least I could go to my bunk safe in the knowledge that my cabin was still my own and my status was still intact. But I was seething at the message Henry had delivered to me; it was as if the outside world had tracked me down and assaulted me in my own home. Unable to sleep, I went out into the night and found I could identify a few more stars now. I started to compose a letter in my head:

Dear Gareth, you won't be disappointed with the footage I have shot. I was surprised to hear that I am no longer your guest…

Just then, I noticed Rob on an inactive drill deck. The grab must have stopped above the wreck, presumably waiting for the lens to clear again before pouncing. The sea was still, and it was a perfect night for watching shooting stars.

"When I'm out here," Rob said, "it feels like nobody else lives on this crowded planet. Up there are millions more planets, and down here is just me."

"And me," I said.

"Yes"—he laughed—"and all of us on this tiny tub floating about in the middle of nowhere."

"I've come to realise that it doesn't matter how old or rusty this tub is; it is all that exists between our lives and the ocean floor."

"Which is why sailors refer to ships as she. Like our mothers, who protect us when we are small."

"I tend to think of a ship as non-gender-related and for a woman to be a woman, not a boat. But perhaps this is churlish, and I should succumb to tradition."

"Perhaps you should," he answered.

I thought about that for a moment. Having seen men on ships longing for a maternal presence, the *she* reference is perhaps not as insulting as it first seems. But there is still an irony in this, since the presence of a real woman on board a ship is thought to bring bad luck, a myth brought about because a woman was thought to be a distraction to the male sailors on board. Rob waited for me to finish my thoughts.

"It's impossible not to love your ship," he said, "because without her, we would drown."

"The *John Barry* didn't protect. She drowned."

"But unlike her crew, she still exists right here beneath us. She keeps the memory of those who sailed in her alive." Rob was enjoying the stars. I hadn't heard him speak like this before.

"So is it the romance of shipwrecks, or is this just about treasure?"

"There is always romance with any shipwreck," he said. "It's why men risk their lives in a way they would only do for their loved ones."

"Like Jay, you mean?"

"Well, yes, he's certainly a romantic. But take Keith Jessop, he was instrumental in the survey vessel finding the location of the *John Barry*. He's quite a character."

"In what way?"

"He's a belligerent Yorkshireman and a pain in the arse, can't be part of a team. We had to get rid of him. But he knows how to find wrecks."

"Go on."

"He's self-taught; that's what is remarkable about him. He was raised in abject poverty and left school at the age of fourteen without a single qualification to his name. He had learned to dive while doing his national service with the Royal Marines. To begin with, he made very little money out of the debris from wrecks in the seas off Scotland. He discovered that there were rewards if you knew where to find them, yet he still managed to spend much of his time in very real danger. He's a nutcase. Diving in a second-hand Royal Navy dry suit, he made for himself a homemade air compressor out of various household appliances, including a washing machine and a vacuum cleaner. He then combined a tractor tyre inner tube with some mesh to make a basket in which to put the spoils. It's a miracle he survived any of his dives. More down to luck than skill or judgement, especially when he began to use underwater explosives in *trial and error* experiments."

"Isn't that what Pierre Valdy attempted on the *John Barry*?"

"Yes, with Jessop, without success. He's like all treasure hunters; he belongs to a particular breed who feel at their most alive when danger, history and reward combine," Rob said with a hint of admiration in his voice. "But he was also not the Salvage Association's favourite salvor."

Apparently, they had reluctantly agreed to give him the rights to search for a wreck that had sunk in the Pentland Firth in Scotland, on the condition that if he returned emptyhanded, there would be no more salvage rights granted to him. Not that any other salvage crew was interested, deeming it to be too dangerous and inaccessible. But Jessop not only found the wreck, he also recovered a vast amount of copper from inside its hold.

This established his reputation as a chief player in the world of treasure hunting. He then turned his focus to the HMS *Edinburgh*, a ship that had been carrying ten tonnes of what was known as *Stalin's Gold* to the Soviet Union during World War II, when she was sunk by a German U-boat.

"Jessop knew roughly the location of the wreck, but to recover it from such depths in the Barents Sea was a massive undertaking. He remortgaged his home to finance the project and made a deal with a prominent North Sea diving contractor. The sea was unbearably cold, and Jessop and his dive team embarked on what was nothing short of a technical nightmare, but they emerged triumphant with more than $100 million worth of gold bullion. That's what makes him the most successful treasure hunter of all time."

"Are you a treasure hunter, Rob?"

"No, not me. I like to run projects and be successful at them. I like to be certain of what I'm doing. Let people like Jessop sell their souls for something that may not exist." Just then, the Major joined us. I didn't imagine that he had much time for the romance of treasure hunting, either. He was a proud professional. He would carry out his duty no matter what.

"A great night for stargazing," he said. "Can you identify Orion?"

"No, I can only admire people who navigate by the stars," I said.

He reached for his binoculars and spent a moment peering through them before handing them to me.

"Look at the moon's gaping craters. They are so bright and defined tonight."

The moon seemed to be suspended just above the silhouette of the derrick, which was swinging gently like a pendulum in the night sky. All perspective is lost at sea. I handed the binoculars to Rob. Silently, he studied the full moon before readjusting them. "That's strange," he said, quietly passing them to the Major.

"Lights on our starboard side quite close."

"That reporter was fast in giving away our location," he retorted.

There followed an eerie pause while the two men peered into the darkness. This was the first unscheduled ship that has been sighted since the tanker the night of the squall.

Pirates? Had they appeared just when I'd stopped looking?

The two men made a dash to the bridge, with me following behind. There, we found the officer on watch already trying to radio the mystery ship. A tense interlude followed. Captain Paul was called for.

"It's too large for pirates," said Rob confidently. Just then, the radio crackled to reveal a container ship on its way from Bombay to the Suez.

"Ha, they would have been just as surprised to see a drill ship in an area not known for drilling," he said, the relief on his face clearly showing.

We watched from the bridge wing as the elevated starboard lights on the merchant vessel glided soundlessly by. Studying the expressions on the faces on the bridge, it was clear that pirates still posed a very real threat to a static target tethered to the bottom of the ocean.

Chapter Twenty-Seven

Rob had been up since 2 am and was in the monitor room. They had been removing the roof of Captain Ellerwald's cabin in pursuit of the safe. The pictures relayed back to us were the clearest they had ever been. This was because we were now right over the aft section of the broken wreck, which was much higher and much less hampered by sediment. As the camera panned along its side, a row of helmets were very clear on the monitor. *There had been no time to put them on.*

Once the operator was sure he had reached the captain's cabin, Rob called Jean Roux, who had only gone to bed an hour and a half before. He returned to his post without complaint, but after several hours of trying to locate the safe, the DPS started playing up again. Frustrated, he made a grab. When the screen cleared, only a sheared-off metal sheet, probably some decking, was revealed. Reluctantly, they concluded that the floor of the cabin was no longer there, perhaps destroyed by the torpedo; in all probabilities, the safe had sunk to the bottom and was encased in white clay. Either way, it could not be found.

Rob's disappointment at not accomplishing his plan and the two days lost searching for the safe was hard for him to hide. Pierre was philosophical, saying we were bound to have some bad days. But the men were weary and frustrated. Instead of the expected euphoria at retrieving one million and four hundred thousand silver coins against all the odds, there was a sense of dissatisfaction. *Always the desire for more.*

Rob turned to Jean Roux. "Well, we'll have to guess Hold One or Hold Four? We don't have enough time to explore both."

"I suggest we go back to the fore deck, to Hold One," replied the impassive Frenchman.

We all knew there was one week left, if that, until the monsoon season. Would we ever find the bullion? Did it even exist? It was easy to move the phantom bars around to other parts of the ship in the name of hope, yet without evidence, it could so easily be a lost cause. Coin fatigue had set in, and an impatience to find more silver had taken over. It seemed that everyone, apart from Rob and possibly Al, who would not commit for he was an observer after all, was convinced that the ingots were there. Or wanted to believe. Rob looked more thoughtful than ever. He was now under pressure to go after them, but he was more inclined to pick up the last of the coins. Inevitably, he was *persuaded* to go in search of the silver bars for I was on a ship of gamblers; why continue with coins when you could gamble on finding an even bigger prize?

The grab returned to the front of the wreck and started removing tonnes of military cargo from the upper decks. Rob continued with his calculations. He asked Al to check some figures regarding the weight and draft of the cargo. Al was of the opinion that the Liberty ship was at capacity so where the bullion would have been stored was still a mystery, but Mac maintained his theory that cargo could have been swapped for the bullion at the last minute. It had been known to happen. He sent telegrams to Brian, who was trying to raise money for twenty extra days on site. Rob thought this was unrealistic with the monsoon season so near. Out of the daily running costs of $50,000, $3,000 of that went on fuel alone. The *Flex LD* had a tank that held a million gallons, and the tank was less than half full now; the engines had been going strong since leaving Singapore more than three months ago. Not to be outdone by the Americans, Sheikh Ahmed said he would raise another $400,000 to fund the extra days. Rob seemed a little deflated by all this talk of bullion and staying longer. He wanted to deliver the coins as that is what he had been employed to do. The Major was not deflated; he was relieved to have finished his counting, and, in any case, he was never deflated. Mac was not deterred either; he believed that the bullion was still there waiting for us and was increasingly excited by the prospect of delving further.

Brad emerged from his cabin, where he was spending more and more time. He claimed that he had been duped into believing that we would find bullion, not just coins.

"All my crew," he protested, "including myself, came cheap on the understanding that there would be bonuses all around when the silver bars were recovered."

"There were no guarantees," Rob said. "That was clear."

"Well, if I were an investor, I would be very unhappy about being taken for a ride," Brad said. His attitude was received with a certain amount of disdain, coming as it did from the man who had dropped three hundred thousand coins into the sea.

No funds from either America or Oman materialised, and the sea was whipping up. Rob announced his decision.

"We will return to Oman and deliver the coins." There were some groans from those who had stood to gain and silent cheers from the Indonesian workers and the men on the bridge as news filtered through. He followed this up with a debrief in the white room.

"We have fulfilled our remit to retrieve the coins. 1.4 million of them." There were some murmurings of discontent that we hadn't found the bullion. But Rob was not moved.

"No need to be downhearted; the operation is a success. I'm positive that the investors are already planning a second expedition." *A second expedition?*

The men's spirits were lifted by this news. Another chase was on the cards. Would I go through it all again? *I would.*

"When?" I asked.

"The next weather window all being well," said Rob.

My heart was beating harder than I would have liked. This had never been the plan, but maybe I had caught the bug too. *I could bring a better camera, more tape stock...* As Jay always said, "Wreck fever never goes away."

"I do not believe the skip is lost forever," said Jean Roux in a rare moment of speaking directly to me. "When we return, we will bring a submersible to retrieve it."

Following the reference to the skip, Brad looked down at the floor and did not mention the bullion again.

Every member of the crew was presented with a coin, plus a certificate of authentication made from old chart paper by one of the Frenchmen on the bridge. Mine had *Mr Bailey Catherine* printed in black on the top right-hand corner. *Got my name right at last. Well, almost.* And I was the proud owner of a silver ryal.

Each segment of the pipe had to be dismantled and stacked on the racks. It would take at least another twenty-four hours before we could leave our position. A last-ditch grab at the bridge retrieved the SS *John Barry's* telegraph and compass, but at a critical moment, the ship heaved and the telegraph was crushed. These last two broken souvenirs of the SS *John Barry* stayed on the monitor for two days until the grab re-emerged, a sad reminder of a Liberty ship that never arrived at her destination.

While lying on my bunk reading Mrs Croft's account of her life at sea, *"...and I can safely say, that the happiest part of my life has been spent on board a ship,"* I realised that, so far, all my filming had been from the perspective of being on board and that I didn't have any shots of the Flex LD from outside. I had arrived in a trance and not filmed our arrival. That seemed an age ago now.

The wind that had raged all night had suddenly dropped, and the sea was unusually calm. I asked Captain Paul if I could go out on the dinghy to film the ship from a distance. He sent the first mate to meet my request.

Even with a calm sea, there was still a heave of about ten feet between the Jacob's ladder and the dinghy. The trick was to time your leap and not to hesitate. The *Flex LD* loomed imperiously above; the two of us balanced ourselves on the rubber sides of the boat and chugged alongside the brightly painted red hull. I remembered with a tremor what it felt like to be so low in the water.

In this part of the world, a lack of wind is accompanied by a furious heat, which immediately burned my arms. I tried to hold the camera steady, but it was almost impossible with the boat rocking from side to side in the swell. I was reminded that no one could last long on an open boat in this heat without shelter. We gained some temporary relief under the massive suspended anchors that cast some shade over us under the bow.

"Want some fun?" said the first mate.

"Of course," I replied.

He pulled at the throttle and spun the dinghy around. We sped freely away from our ocean home, which diminished in size the further we flew. The only way to ride the rollers was to crouch and bend our knees like shock absorbers as we bounced into the air. At full speed, we were flying above the waves like flying fish, leaping higher and falling harder, drenching ourselves in spray and yelling at the top of our voices.

The whole of the Indian Ocean is ours.

Finally, we were an untethered ship again. We set sail at night, our booty safely secured below. The bow cut through the ocean, spraying salt and wind through our hair. Cut loose from their shackles, crew and ship were one. *We are free.*

The stars appeared as they used to, unthreatening and passive, very different from the ones that had smothered me on the dhow. We were returning to the land of familiarity, where the stars are distant and the earth is populated. No more sea boots and hard hats; it was back to suits and ties, jeans and shorts. We would no longer be marooned on a little piece of iron cut loose in the ocean.

An *end-of-run* party atmosphere took hold while outside the wind increased. A storm was forecast. Down in the mess, courtesy of Captain Paul, champagne was poured, and there were no restrictions on beer.

Tom showed a completely different side to his personality by juggling oranges and singing at the top of his voice. The Major joined him with a dirty rugby song, much to the amusement of those who could understand, before breaking into *Jerusalem*, which the French attempted to drown out with an anti-British song from the Napoleonic wars. It was unusual to see Al in the mess. He was standing impassively as the rowdiness increased. Finally, he came over to speak to me.

"Well, goodnight," he said. It was his way of saying goodbye. There was a long pause as we stood looking at each other. I wondered about asking him to dance. "I just want you to know," he went on, "that you tell people things at sea that you never would anywhere else."

"Understood," I said. *For tomorrow, we will be on land.*

Eric bravely sang his Dutch song that nobody understood, and Mac sang a solo rendition of a ditty that incorporated all fifty states of America. The Filipinos insisted on us each dancing to one refrain of a guitar played by the cook, revealing another one of his talents. The rest of the crew looked on until it was discovered that the two songs in which all the nationalities were able to join in were *Yellow Submarine* and *La Bamba*, possibly the two worst songs ever recorded. I was lifted onto a table to dance the night away.

By the time the party had reached a crescendo of noise and high spirits, it was hard to imagine that outside the monsoon had arrived, and we were hurtling towards land. Our time was over. And the beleaguered SS *John Barry* could once again lie in peace.

As the party rumbled on and the liquor took hold, there was a change in some of the men's attitude towards me. There was a definite shift from the strict rules that had been applied so far. They were being released from their duties, and with that, I sensed a danger I hadn't experienced before. Who was I anyway? This lone woman on their ship? And why hadn't I slept with any of them? The Major was particularly sharp as always. His grin was wider than ever.

"Come on," he said, "so many men to choose from, who takes your fancy?"

"Yes," Tom said, "you can have any of us. Take your pick."

The Major winked knowingly at me. "I suspect none of them."

"Something like that," I said, and with that, I made myself scarce. It was time to be out of sight. Moving swiftly towards the make-shift bar, I made my escape out of a side door. I was careful not to be followed, and instead of making for my cabin, I turned and ran up the metal staircase that I had been up and down so many times in the past few months. I made my way to the dark and silent bridge, where two sober officers on watch were content to be pitching through the night and on the move again. We scanned the black velvet void ahead of us, not a ship's light to be seen. The magnetism of the sea is so powerful that it tries to prevent you from ever re-entering the land of people. *The world is a crowded place until you are crossing an ocean.*

Chapter Twenty-Eight

For the second time in my life, I entered the sleepy harbour of Raysut at dawn, this time from a much higher vantage point. After unloading its valuable cargo, the *Flex LD* would return to France, making the magnificent journey through the Suez Canal and across the Mediterranean. *How I wish I could go with them.* They would be afforded the time to reflect and attune to the climate and culture changes ahead. Air travel, on the other hand, collides with the time that is needed for the mind to adjust from one culture to another. One thing the British military learned from the Falklands War was that there was a greater prevalence of mental health issues in Army soldiers, many of whom were flown home at the end of the conflict, compared to the Royal Marines, who sailed home slowly and had time to decompress before being thrust back into the normality of civilian life. But I was a disposable expense, and there was no way Gareth would agree to me enjoying any more of their hospitality.

I looked around the empty hospital room, where I had spent many hours trying to make sense of my life. I folded my tattered clothes and placed them inside my rucksack. I put my trusty camera that Wayne had so painstakingly restored into its bag. I had decided to leave before the party people were awake. Mac was still sleeping. He planned to spend more time in Salalah. He wanted to explore those lush green mountains again before returning to the hubbub of Washington. I didn't want any drawn-out goodbyes. I passed a few of the crew in the corridor outside the mess; some stopped for a hug and to tell me that I was a jolly good sport. But men in port look very different from the men you knew at sea.

At dawn, all was quiet as ropes were thrown over the bollards on the empty wharf. Rob and the Major, on duty to the last, were standing attentively by the crane as it dipped into the hold extracting the first crates of coins and placing them carefully on the quay. They were lit by a shaft of orange light from the sun as it clawed its way over the mountaintops. We were distracted by a small plane flying low above us and landing nearby. It was very obviously not a commercial one.

Come to spirit the silver away.

It was time for me to go. I was a solitary figure tottering down the gangplank trying to find my sea legs before I made a fool of myself. Not that anyone was looking on as the work continued above me. I stood on the wharf and gazed upward, trying to smile bravely. I waved a pathetic wave, like a child leaving home for the first time. I wanted to run back up the gangplank and lie on my bunk.

"See you in Blighty," called Rob. "I look forward to watching the film."

Yes, the film. I still have to make a film. I shivered at the thought. *Where to begin?* The precious cargo would take several hours to unload and transfer onto the plane, watched carefully by Rob and the Major. My job now was to somehow make sense of the tiny tapes I was carrying. They were *my* precious cargo.

"See you in Columbia!" the Major shouted.

"Columbia?"

"Yes, aren't you coming with me? Make a good movie."

"I think I'd better make this one first," I said, patting my camera bag, "but thanks for the offer."

"Until next time," he called after me as I tried to look purposeful, striding up to the wire gates that led me back into the world of rocks and sand.

I left behind their optimism. This mission was far from over. After all, the secrets of the SS *John Barry*'s cargo had to be revealed sometime. The bullion hidden in their minds was still there waiting for them, along with the coins lost in the basket, the catch that got away. They were not going to give up until they had recovered every last piece of treasure.

But when the chase is over, *what then?* There *has* to be more because no treasure is ever enough because, in the end, it is just pieces of silver.

Chapter Twenty-Nine

If I had been reluctant to leave my bare hospital quarters inside the seven thousand tonnes of rust and grease that had been my home for the past three months, I was even more hesitant about leaving Oman. In Muscat, Henry did not mention staying with him, and, in any case, I knew he would try and prevent me from doing what I had always wanted to do ever since arriving in the country. I found myself a car to drive. I had secretly longed for the journey the Major had invited me to go on, one that ventured deep into the desert, but I wanted to go alone. I wanted to be me once more. Not the Catherine who had played a role for so long. The joker, the counsellor, the good-time girl who could hold her own in banter, could even dance on a table when called upon. I wanted time to process my experience, to reflect and to be ready for my journey home. The Indian Ocean had tried to swallow me up. I had almost disappeared without a trace, but I had been saved. Time had not given up on me just yet.

And now I wanted time that was mine. And mine alone.

Leaving the Muscat traffic behind, I turned onto the Nakhl Road, where there were no cars at all. Just the odd warning sign of a camel crossing the road. As I had discovered in Salalah, with so much wealth in Oman, the main roads are perfectly tarmacked and well preserved as there are so few vehicles travelling on them.

The Nakhl Road wound up through the rock-strewn desert towards the shimmering mountains, where the temperature reaches over fifty degrees in the summer. Nestled amongst the foothills, Nakhl Fort came into view. Newly restored and the colour of red sandstone, it flashed its importance at me. A right-angled turn off the highway led me straight into Nakhl, where I drove through the main square to the fort and got out of the car.

A drinking water tanker was supplying one of the houses nearby. Here, water costs more than oil and is the most precious of all the elements. The one-storey dwellings had very small windows to keep them cool and were decorated with elaborately crafted doors and shutters carved out of old olive trees. Some hens were pecking the red sandy ground with seemingly nothing to scrape on. Children ran and hid themselves from me. Three women fetching water from a well were hardly visible in their black as they walked in the shade. They covered their faces when they saw me and hurried by; when I greeted them, they giggled behind their veils. Some men waved, and I waved back as more children ran across the square. Older uniformed children carrying their books on their heads passed me on their way from school. The girls' uncovered faces were shyly observing me. A couple of them half-heartedly threw stones in my direction, but I could see they were more embarrassed than threatening, while the boys, more confident, shook my hand. More and more children surrounded me. I asked one of them how many children attended the school.

"Five hundred," he replied proudly.

A few years ago, there would not have been a school there at all; now there were five hundred children being educated in this one small town.

I continued my drive and was soon curling up the side of a mountain and into a dense plantation of date palms, where I discovered the source of all the greenery. A falaj was irrigating the ground. A falaj is a manmade channel dug in the earth to source any groundwater under the soil. As I emerged from the palms, I turned the car around to look back over the town. All was still.

With the engine off, I sat for a moment with the scorching heat from the sun pinging off the bonnet. I could hardly touch the steering wheel as it soaked up the intense heat of the midday sun, which set the fort ablaze. And it was still only winter.

A mile further on, I joined a dirt road. I was intrigued to follow it further into the mountains. I saw no cars or any vehicles of any type. The road became steeper. As I wound my way through the sheared-off mountain rocks and along waterless streams, I was relieved to see the sign for Al Wabi ahead of me. The village appeared to be asleep, with its few shops closed for the afternoon. One was a small dwelling that called itself a *supermarket* with a few faded photos in the window. I continued on my way through the dry riverbeds and ravines into the mountains. I stopped by a particularly outstanding wadi in that it was actually filled with water mirroring the cloudless sky, besides which some boys were playing football. I drove further into the desert. The terrain became less irrigated and more like the sandy desert I had flown over a few days before.

Arabia. The land of Thesiger, *The Arabian Nights* and T. E. Lawrence. I half expected to see one of them riding towards me. Instead, I came across some bedu who called me over to join them. I was treated as an honorary man sitting on the sand in front of their tents. We had no language, but we smiled while their women brought us dates and sweet coffee before sitting to one side. They were clearly discussing me. They pointed and giggled. The men took no notice of them.

That night, I settled down to sleep in the car. The desert became very cold, but the stars watched over me from far away, and the solitude was comforting.

The following morning, I began my return. Sometimes I waved at men riding camels beside the road but never once saw another car. By evening, I was nearing the outskirts of Muscat. I drew up outside an interesting-looking house; it was at least a hundred years old. It was very unusual to see such an old building, at least by Omani standards, as age is not a symbol of wealth yet; to me, it was by far the most stylish house I had seen in Oman. But then I had grown up with a British craving for the past.

A stunningly pretty young bedu man wearing the traditional Omani dishdasha appeared from behind a heavy, ornately hand-engraved wooden door and invited me to follow him. Inside was a grassy courtyard. The coarse blades crunched beneath my feet as I followed him around the sweet-smelling almond tree that was taking centre stage.

From within the house wafted a powerful aroma. Frankincense burns in many places in Oman, its sweet smell a reminder of a fertile history long before the white modern buildings turned up to demolish the memory. My own memory was of the parish priest tottering down the aisle, swinging his censer, the fragrance drifting over me. *Fanning me towards heaven.*

We both took off our shoes, as is the custom when entering a private home. Abstract paintings and antique cabin chests were the backdrop to a band of men sitting cross-legged on a rug. Here I was introduced to my host, a young, smiling Omani man called Malik. He was sitting with Daniel, an expat from England who was enjoying a gin and tonic and the current company. There's something desperate about the men who want to believe they are still part of an empire, where the Englishman has a *special* relationship with the bedu. They are, in reality, the leftovers of the empire, joking and flirting with young Arab boys.

Daniel was friendly but did not ask how I had suddenly appeared there. Malik sprang to his feet to greet me. He spoke perfect English.

"Welcome to my house. Where are you from?"

"London."

"Ah, London. I know London and New York. Very good clubs. Would you like a drink? Or perhaps a tour of my house?"

"Both would be nice," I said.

He waved towards the bedu man, who had been looking on silently, and he promptly poured me a large gin. Once more, I followed my guide. He had a magnetic charm and an inherent politeness that seemed customary whenever I encountered a Bedouin. He was very thorough in conducting me throughout the rooms, making sure that I saw everything, including a second crenulated walled garden from which we climbed some outside steps to Malik's bedroom. Malik's bedroom was unsurprisingly ornate. Next to it was the bedu's room, devoid of all furniture apart from a bed. I asked him where he came from, and he told me his family was in Sur and that he stayed with Malik during the week. I wanted to ask him if he had a wife and family but fell shy of the question.

We stood for a moment on the top of a parapet, transfixed by the intensity of the stars that once more hung so near that their Arabian magic tricked me into losing all sense of space. A shooting star hurtled across the sky in a flaming ball, producing a firework display all of its own millions of miles away. One star was particularly powerful, as if it were about to lead us to Bethlehem. I was a captive, no longer connected to the world I once knew.

"Stars," I said out loud involuntarily. How banal that sounded now that I was on land once more. But the young bedu nodded sagely, distantly, as if he were part of some larger secret that, if I leaned towards him a little, I might just be able to touch.

Chapter Thirty

I hung back, breathing in one last gasp of desert air. Would I ever again experience the total silence that burns your ears or the stillness where not even a whisper of wind touches your face?

Back in Muscat, Henry was agitated by my absence. He was anxious for me to return to London and get our company going and the *John Barry* film distributed worldwide. He was annoyed that I had taken myself off to the desert with the prized video tapes that were waiting to reveal to the world our story. But I did not care. I wouldn't have missed my moment under the stars with the young bedu, not for anything.

I boarded a 737, and in a matter of hours, a huge heavy cabin door was being opened at Heathrow, and a familiar cold grey air whistled around the fuselage, smelling of aviation fuel and the River Thames.

I had not written to anyone about my voyage or how close I had been to never coming home.

"I had an adventure on a dhow," I told my sister when we were alone.

"I know," she said, "we get the Lloyds List in my office." She was working for a shipping magazine at the time. "It reported that a supply boat on its way to a recovery vessel searching for a World War II wreck in the Indian Ocean failed to arrive. All the men were presumed dead."

"Clearly, no women presumed then?"

"You're an idiot. I was terrified, and of course I didn't tell Mum." She couldn't decide whether to be cross or happy. Both emotions being the same thing when the person you feared was dead is still alive.

"Ah well, sometimes ignorance is bliss," I said, brushing it off.

"Typical," she said.

But the truth was that my treasure-seeking trip to Arabia could have been over before it began. I decided not to let my thoughts dwell on a story that might have ended that way. We didn't refer to it again.

Jane Austen had led me to the edge, but she also returned me safely to where I belonged. I visited her home in Chawton, where her manuscripts preside in glass cases – manuscripts she could not imagine would reach so many readers, or even be read at all, let alone provide solace to a lone female in the midst of the Indian Ocean.

I made a half-hearted attempt at a coming-home party, to which I invited my theatre friends. Naturally, they were full of the latest theatre talk, which I found to be oddly reassuring. Occasionally, I would murmur something about being glad to be alive, and a question would be asked.

"What do you mean?" And then I had no clue where to begin.

My brothers at sea would have understood, but they were a long way away now. Camaraderie is not something that can really be appreciated until it is experienced. It is a result of collective endeavour. I had had highs in the theatre when I had experienced this and again with the men I had spent time with at sea. But at sea, it can also play tricks on the mind when marooned far from a familiar world. A curious malaise takes hold, the longing for something that does not exist, such as the castle in men's minds as described to me on the plastic chairs of the monkey deck. They were lucky; for them, there was always the next voyage, the next venture out to sea, where they could, once more, romanticise about their fictional homes. Not for them, the empty office from where I would have to go on pitching and selling ideas, most of them ending up in a filing cabinet, until one was commissioned and I was set free with a camera once more.

News desks everywhere bought my footage of the millions of coins spilling over the deck. But nobody wanted to buy the documentary about the journey. I called the broadcasters to tell them about the film, but to no avail. I called Channel Four, who had shown some interest in what seemed like an age ago.

"Yes," they said, "we saw it on the news. But it has happened now, and we are concentrating more on events coming up for next year." The film that had been all-important to me seemed of little value now. *But life is of value.*

Henry phoned me one morning while I was still asleep. I was used to receiving his long, florid faxes banged out on the old typewriter I'd seen so often in his flat in Muscat, black ribbon straining to turn as he hit the keys with a passion. Or was it anger? It was hard to tell. I suspect the speed of his ringed fingers hitting the keys had more to do with the excitement of relaying his news to whoever was reading it. But the messages to me were more in the vein of disguised fury, so it was with some surprise that I picked up the phone to hear not an angry voice but his more usual courteous tone.

"Hello, Henry, how are you?"

"I am very well," he replied. "His Royal Highness sends his regards."

"Thank you, please relay mine to him."

To pre-empt his next question, I said, "Isn't it amazing how all the news stations have shown our footage?"

"Yes, excellent. Excellent. Sheikh Ahmed is wondering when he might see the film he is in."

"Yes, I'm working on that," I replied with conviction.

I was not altogether not telling the truth. In the wake of the SS *John Barry's* recovery operation's success, the Omanis invested in a salvage company called *Blue Water Recoveries*, to be run by Rob, with a view to explore more treasure hunting opportunities. Much to my relief, they asked me to make a promo video of the *John Barry* story. I leapt at this chance to redeem myself, only to be told that no dhows were to be included in the film, nor arguments or mishaps, which meant leaving out the dropping of the skip as well. The video needed to demonstrate the technical achievement of the enterprise and promote the sale of the coins. Naturally, I made sure the handsome sheikh was included in the film.

I put together the technical data and supplemented it with diagrams and animation and added narration. I edited late into the night. When I played it back, I had to admire what a technical achievement it had been to retrieve over a million coins from such depths. It was a good story, but not my story. I was paid £10,000 for the video, which I invested in my company and went on to produce more films of my own.

The coins were taken to Switzerland to be auctioned. Some were sold individually in special presentation packs. But there was no bulk buy. It was decided to melt them down so that the ones that did survive were more valuable. There would be some silver bars, after all.

Blue Water Recoveries decided to buy the *Flex LD* rather than continue to lease it from TravOcean. They bought it for $4 million and renamed it the *Deep Sea Worker* in 1995. Rob invited me to make another video for them, and I flew to Portugal to witness the retrieval of gold bars from the RMS *Douro*, a British passenger liner that was sunk in a collision in 1882.

It all felt very different from my last excursion. We were not far off the coast, and the ship was manned by a different crew. There was a lot of serious hosing down to wash the mud off the gold bars that lay side by side on the deck. Beneath us were the invisible graves of the fifty-nine souls who had drowned in the collision.

It was the men who I missed. There was no Wayne or Brad or the twinkling Major. No smiling Mac or the flamboyant Richard. And the other men I had grown so close to faded into a memory along with the treasure hunters with whom I had shared the banter, the laughter, the disappointments and the euphoria. Faded too was that person in the desert taking coffee with the bedu beneath the dazzling sun and the stars. I had done my time with treasure hunting, and so I returned to the world of actors and make believe where I belonged. There was only so much washing of gold that I could film.

The *Deep Sea Worker* made subsequent recoveries from other wrecks but nothing on the scale of the SS *John Barry*. Within a few years, the ship was sold for a massive $36 million, refurbished and converted into a drill ship again, before being scrapped.

But my story didn't end here. I could no longer go on hiding and masking from my friends. If I had learned anything out there in the Indian Ocean, it was *if you are not yourself, then who are you?* Within a couple of years, I met and married a woman, and we had two sons together. Mac was the best man at our wedding. The irony was not lost on Rob when I met up with him and told him. Seeing him without his sea boots, wearing a suit standing in the foyer of a London hotel, I hardly recognised him. He was genuinely pleased for me and introduced me to his young wife and children.

I still have my coin and the marine's helmet. I found it tough dispensing with the hard hat and boots because they retained the smell of those greasy gangways, which, for a long time after, I found weirdly comforting. My copy of *Persuasion* sleeps peacefully on my bookshelf. Occasionally, I will take it down to browse.

> "I hate to hear you talk about all women as if they were fine ladies instead of rational creatures. None of us want to be in calm waters all our lives."

Sometimes I dream of a wreck being smashed to pieces by a giant grab while still defiantly guarding her secret. And in that dream, a flying fish darts from out of the deep into my hands and delivers a reminder to be myself, which becomes more pertinent with each passing year, for lost in the sea of time is a memory that not even a boat-tossing squall can ever blow away.

Post Script

Once more, I find myself the only woman, this time at a table of men in a London restaurant. We meet in a pub in Piccadilly. As no one has a clue where to go eat, I lead them to Vasco and Piero's in Soho. Here, we sit at a large, round table and order prosecco and pasta. Not seventy-five men this time, but seven men and me.

Opposite me is Mac, now in his fifties and still representing the remains of the JB4, which consists of the offspring of Jay and Brian, who are now dead. Richard (Riccardo to his friends) has left Mac to broker a new deal; he appears to have lost interest in the whole enterprise but still stands to make a lot of money if the bullion is ever found.

Gareth is there, more bent over now, but his eyes are as keen as ever, darting about the room, avoiding mine. He declines the prosecco and asks for fizzy water, for after years of colonial drinking, he is now teetotal. Seated next to me is Rob Hudson; his tan is a little faded but his soft eyes are still framed by the spikey blonde hair, now tinged with grey. He is an immediate comfort given the unexpected circumstances in which we find ourselves. He and Gareth alone now represent the Ocean Group, as Sheikh Ahmed has also died in the interim years.

The men who survived are still searching for the treasure that survived. They are older and wearier, but treasure hunters never retire. They go on with their everlasting search for gold and silver. And so, here they are again. Ready to go.

Twenty-five years after the recovery of the coins, a new expedition is planning to return to the site. The unsolved mystery of the silver bullion makes the SS *John Barry* one of history's most intriguing treasure ships, and it remains in the top ten of most valuable wrecks of all time. It was never going to be left in peace.

A party based in Singapore has joined the group. They are listening to Mac's banter with Gareth. "Tell me, Gareth, now that we are friends again, would you save me if I was kidnapped in Yemen?"

"Well, I would have had you taken there in the first place," he says, "put a price on your head, then taken a cut before having you rescued. So, yes."

There is much laughter. *Some a little nervous.*

The founder of the Singapore company is referred to only as RJ; his assistant is taking notes, his modest portion of pasta untouched. RJ has spent fifteen years researching the wreck of the SS *John Barry* and has become obsessed with a desire to uncover the holds we never had time to reach and to delve much deeper inside. *Ali Baba's Cave.*

He claims to have new evidence as to the whereabouts of the silver bars – not that he will disclose more than that, but he is already raising the financial investment needed for the new venture. At the mention of investment, our gathering becomes animated and more prosecco is ordered.

If the man from Singapore is right, then all the men I am looking at are going to become very rich men indeed. Rob is more interested in the project itself. He explains that the expedition will not be the same as before. The world has changed. The salvage vessel will be significantly less expensive as it is much smaller than the *Flex LD,* with a crew of a mere ten instead of seventy-five. But the bond required by the United States government to ensure that no pollutants are spilled and marine life is protected is astronomical in comparison. Gone are the days of smashing wrecks and spilling marine oil into the ocean. *Let's hope anyway.*

The seven men are not deterred. Gareth, now in full flow, is heartily regaling stories about life in the Middle East. He points a couple of deliberately sexist quips at me to test my reaction. I laugh them off because that is my way of dealing with him.

"No women this time!" *Hilarious. Same old Gareth.*

"We'll see about that!" I answer, but he looks away.

It is good to be next to Rob again, even though this time we have no stars to gaze at, just waiters filling our glasses and bringing us copious amounts of pasta. After all these years, Rob is still disturbed about the missing skip.

"There was no reason not to attach more cables before letting the grab release it." He shakes his head. "We definitely had stronger cables on board."

He has gone over this in his mind many times and thinks now that maybe he should have been less tolerant and released Brad of his duties at the time.

"I would still like to see that skip recovered," he says sadly. The mission is not closed, as far as he is concerned, until it is found. He is now seventy-nine.

He is very fit, still climbing mountains and keen as ever, but still seeking evidence when it comes to the bullion.

Nobody can answer that question. There is only one way to find out.

Mac toasts the SS *John Barry* and the new venture, and we all join in together. Rob tells Gareth I am writing a book about our last expedition, to which he replies fiercely to him and not to me, whom he once again avoids.

"She cannot do that because she doesn't have the rights to the story."

But Mac, ever the lawyer, interjects on my behalf. "I think she is entitled to tell her own story," he says. Gareth grunts and drinks his water.

As we gather by the door of the Italian restaurant, Gareth puts on his coat, and without a goodbye to any of us, he disappears into the cold winter's night.

"Well, goodbye, Gareth," Mac says to the empty street outside. "If it's the cheque you are worried about, I've already paid it."

We stand on the corner of Berwick Street and look at each other.

"Well, then," Rob says, "I suppose it's back to the Indian Ocean to pick up the silver bullion that we seem to have left behind."

Mac turns to me, full of smiles. "Yes, and you, Catherine, have to come with us. It will be an adventure."

Oman

Me and the *Flex LD*

Outside toilet in Dhow   Owner of the Dhow

Attaching pipes to the drill string   Derrick with drill string

Grab with coins

Lowering coins into the hold

Packing the coins

Fixing ropes to the tray

Bag of coins

Silver Ryals

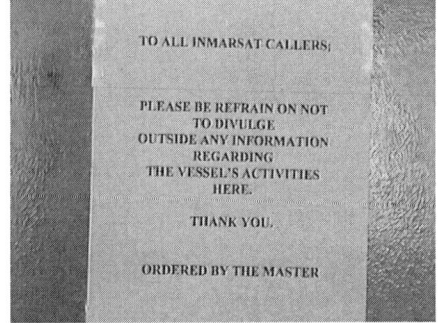

Last night on board

Notice to crew

Major David Hopps

Wayne

Pierre Valdy

Rob and me

Brian, Mac, me and Jay

Al on the Helipad

Mac and the Dhow

On land again

Oman Road